The Research Project: How to write it

The Research Project: How to write it

RALPH BERRY

London and New York

First published 1966 as *How to Write a Research Paper*
by Pergamon Press
Second edition published 1986

Third edition first published 1994
by Routledge
11 New Fetter Lane, London EC4P 4EE

Simultaneously published in the USA and Canada
by Routledge
29 West 35th Street, New York, NY 10001

Reprinted 1995 (twice)

© 1994 Ralph Berry

Typeset in 10/12 pt Times New Roman
Printed and bound in Great Britain by
T. J. Press (Padstow) Ltd, Padstow, Cornwall

British Library Cataloguing in Publication Data
A catalogue record for this book is available from the British Library

Library of Congress Cataloguing in Publication Data
A catalogue record for this book is available from the Library of Congress

ISBN 0–415–11090–4

Contents

Introduction

This guide is intended as an introduction to the research paper. It is designed to be relevant to students at all levels of higher education. The techniques discussed are such as must be employed in even the simplest research assignment, and in the more demanding tasks that students may have to face later in their careers.

The terms of reference of this assignment may vary widely. It may be called a research paper, a thesis or even a dissertation. Its objective may be a neutral compilation of fact, or the achievement of original conclusions. Its length may range from two to upwards of ten thousand words. But the central situation remains unchanged; the writer will be expected to demonstrate a mastery of the scholarly disciplines. These may be defined as the ability to draw on a reasonably wide range of recognized authorities; to learn something of the techniques of getting the most out of a library system; to sustain the labour of taking accurate notes over a long period; to digest them into a shapely and lucid whole; and to present them with due respect for the acknowledged conventions of documentation. At all levels these remain the major concerns of the researcher.

The acquisition of these scholarly skills is, for American first-year college students, the subject of a specific course, usually lasting half a session. The course is a formal requirement and is backed by a wide selection of excellent manuals. British students, by contrast, are most unlikely to receive more than a little token instruction, but rather are expected to pick it up as they go along. The American manuals, some of which may be available to them, are not always relevant to the British educational system, or to the resources available to British students. Yet the preparation of a research paper (let us say, in practice, a paper that goes distinctly beyond the limits of a normal essay) is increasingly a feature of the student scene here, as it has long been in the United States. My aim in writing this guide is to provide the necessary guidance in a straightforward and readable form.

In writing it, I have made certain assumptions that I should now make clear.

1.   I am not concerned with basic composition, and have no intention of telling my readers how to write sentences. The development of a coherent

1

argument, however, is, I feel, so much a part of the research paper that I discuss it in Chapters 4 and 5. But otherwise I assume that my readers will turn to manuals of English composition for any guidance that they may need in that field.

2. I assume that the researcher needs, not simply a series of imperatives and recommendations, but the reasons for the recommendations. Working by rote can never lead to first-class research. Accordingly, I have tried, as far as seemed feasible, to justify the advice I give; and to consider the perfectly reasonable objections that a student might well make, if present to discuss the point with me.

3. Next, I am not concerned with purely scientific and technical areas of research. These require a specialized and formal type of report, which is outside the scope of this manual.

4. This guide was conceived as an introduction to the research paper; and I have sometimes been in some doubt as to what should be left to common sense. At the risk of rightly offending some of my readers, I have on occasion included material that might well have been left unwritten. For example, it sounds banal to advise readers to keep a photocopy, or backup disk, of their work. I know and I apologize. But I have known students to whom the advice would have been useful.* I do not see why experience has to be, as Bismarck termed it, 'the name we give to our mistakes'. It can be passed on. I have applied one simple test on issues of superfluous advice. I have asked myself: 'Would it have been useful to me, as a student?' If the answer is yes, in it goes.

5. Finally, I assume that all papers will be presented in typescript. This is now widely recognized as the only acceptable medium for presenting a paper, but I wish to draw attention to its symbolic importance. Handwriting belongs to the sphere of personal communication. To the argument that handwriting 'shows character', the short answer is that character should be revealed, if at all, by the choice of words, not the style of handwriting. Absence of handwriting implies the acceptance of an impersonal code of conventions. The conventions and techniques embodied in a research paper will be of general and enduring value, beyond the college level. The sort of person to whom all reports are submitted — research supervisor, chief executive, editor — is interested primarily in the content, presented in a frictionless medium. Typescript admits implicitly this situation.

The matter of typing reveals in part the whole philosophy for the

---

*We all need to learn at some point. The distinguished historian, A. J. P. Taylor, writes of himself: 'I received no instruction how to conduct research. I was not even warned to put down the number of the document I was copying, which caused me a great deal of unnecessary work later.' A. J. P. Taylor, 'Accident Prone or What Happened Next', *Encounter*, Vol. 49 (October 1977), pp. 53–61 (p. 54).

research paper. The key words in this philosophy are organization, discipline, and convention. These words may not be wholly welcome to all my readers, and I should perhaps offer a gloss on them. For most students, the English essay will have been strongly associated in the past with imagination, creativity, self-expression, and a somewhat loose approach to form. These are perfectly proper concepts, which have an excellent educational justification. I merely point out that they are irrelevant here. Yet, in my experience, students tend to carry over into the realm of the research paper attitudes and aims, formed in the field of creative writing, that have no place in research. The kind of writing for which this guide is designed, on the contrary, is concerned with the critical assessment of existing authorities. The philosophy, then, can be defended thus. Organization is necessary for the efficient allocation of one's time and effort, and for the presentation of a paper whose internal structure is balanced and sound, and whose argument proceeds along logical lines. Discipline is central to the long labour of sifting authorities, and adding one's own critical comments only when these authorities have been fully assimilated. Conventions are vital in a context where one writes not for oneself, but for a critical public — a public whose face may change (professor, departmental head, director) but whose standards remain approximately the same. The student will address the paper to such people, and ultimately may join them. And this is the true justification of conventions, that they offer freedom of movement within a larger group. Students need not fear that these tedious conventions are cramping: ultimately they will serve to free the power of expression.

CHAPTER 1

The Choice of Subject: Using the Library

In this and the following chapters I intend to consider the problems of the research paper in the order in which they present themselves to the student. The first — and, to my mind, by far the greatest — problem is the choice of subject and, more particularly, of title. The general area of study is hardly a problem. A field of study, such as the 1914–18 poets, or automation, or the psychology of aesthetics, is selected or assigned. Three thousand words, say, have to be written on a topic in which the student is presumably interested. But at this stage the student is nowhere near fixing a *title* for the paper. It is clear that 'Automation', for example, is unacceptable as a title. It is far too broad. The topic will have to be defined and limited after some preliminary reading, preferably in consultation with the student's supervisor. Even then the title may well have to remain provisional. Suppose one originally started with the vague idea of 'Automation', and, after some preliminary reading, reduced it by stages to 'Automation in Britain', to 'The Impact of Automation on British Industry in the 1970s'. Even this might, on further reading, prove to be too broad a topic to handle adequately within the limits of the paper. One might well finish up with 'The Impact of Automation on Office Industry in Britain in the 1970s'. The title, true, is getting longer and clumsier. But it does promise to deliver certain quite specific goods.

Here, then, is perhaps the first lesson of research; it can, in a very general way, be planned, but not blueprinted. One simply does not know what one is going to discover. These discoveries may lead to a complete change of direction. So be it: but at least this possibility should be taken into account in the planning stage. It is, then, desirable to limit one's topic *as soon as possible* to eliminate wasteful and unproductive reading; but one has to keep the title provisional as long as possible. The sheer pressure of notes and ideas has a way of imposing its own limitations, or even indicating its own path. The student's own developing interest in one area of the subject may also be a vital factor.

Then again, the formal objective of the paper has to be clarified at once. There is, strictly, a distinction between a *report*, which simply relates facts in neutral fashion, and a *thesis*, which definitely seeks to draw conclusions and assert an evaluation of the material. In practice this distinction tends to be blurred. Unless otherwise stated in the terms of reference, there is no reason why the student should not draw conclusions from the material studied. The whole matter of purpose, however, is one to be taken up with the supervisor at the beginning of the assignment. Since this purpose will inform and limit the labour of several weeks or months, its importance needs no emphasizing. I recommend a thorough discussion of the purpose with the student's supervisor, at the very beginning of the assignment.

The process, then, is one of restriction. A field is narrowed down to a title, which itself states or implies the objective of the research. One further factor has to be considered before the final decision on the title has hardened. It is useless to embark on a project before satisfying oneself that an adequate range of sources is at hand. The value of any work of research depends almost entirely on the sources used, a thought one might well bear in mind before starting on a fascinating but, as yet, little documented field like, say, 'The effect of surrogate parenthood on marriage and the family', or 'The dissolution of the U.S.S.R.'. Even with less immediately contemporary topics, one has to ask a few brutally realistic questions. Have the books (or papers) actually been written on the subject? If so, are they available in the college library? Will it be necessary to travel to another, better-equipped, library? Can one take a book out there, or is it necessary to take notes on the spot?

Clearly, the whole issue of choosing a subject makes little sense until it is related to the available sources. The chief source-gathering area is normally the college library. So far, I have treated the issue on the theoretical plane, but in fact it will be determined by the practical situation. It is high time to consider the practice of the matter.

Using the Library

The students' first task will be to acquaint themselves fully with the resources of their own college or university library. The logical place to start is with the library staff and the information they can provide.

The Library Staff

Making the acquaintance of the library staff is a high priority for any researcher. They know all about the facilities of the library and it is folly to neglect the personal channels to the sources. They can usually supply printed or duplicated handout material, offering a useful guide to the library's layout and particular features. This will include important information on special collections, which may be separately housed and catalogued. It will also give information on the particular methods used for cataloguing in the library, and on such matters as CD ROMs, microform materials, thesis abstracts, photocopying facilities, availability of computers and computer data bases, etc. The library may have specialist librarians who can offer assistance with bibliographic work and information services. Increasingly libraries are becoming much more than collections of books and, to obtain the fullest benefit from them, the student should not hesitate to consult the library staff. I have invariably found librarians to be courteous and helpful, indeed most anxious that their library should be efficiently used. The librarian is the expert and the expert should be consulted.

The Open Shelves

Contact having been made with the librarian, students may feel that the obvious place to begin research is the open shelves. Certainly a familiarity with their layout is essential. There are two principal classifications: the Dewey Decimal System and the Library of Congress Classification.

(a) *The Dewey Decimal System* classifies books according to the following broad scheme:

000–099	General Works
100–199	Philosophy and Psychology
200–299	Religion
300–399	Social Sciences
400–499	Languages
500–599	Pure Sciences
600–699	Technology : Applied Sciences
700–799	Fine Arts and Recreation
800–899	Literature
900–999	General Geography, History and Travel
F	Fiction in English

These broad categories are further subdivided. For example Literature is divided thus:

800	Literature
810	American Literature
820	English Literature
830	German Literature
840	French Literature
850	Italian Literature
860	Spanish Literature
870	Latin Literature
880	Greek Literature
890	Minor Literatures

These categories are then further broken down. English Literature, for example, is redivided thus:

821   Poetry
822   Drama
823   Fiction
824   Essays
825   Oratory
826   Letters
827   Satire and Humour
828   Miscellany
829   Anglo-Saxon Literature

Each of these broad groups is then further divided by the use of three decimal places, to give ever more gradations of subject matter. To find the exact placement of a book on the shelves quickly, students may also find it helpful to know the practice of many large libraries of assigning a book an additional author classification. The book *Graven Images* by Allen I. Ludwig, for example, has the Dewey Decimal number 718 and the additional author number L966g. Fairly obviously, this is derived from the first letter of the author's surname, plus various numbers standing for other letters of the alphabet.

(b) *The Library of Congress Classification* has the large groupings of subjects lettered as follows:

A   General Works – Polygraphy
B   Philosophy – Religion
C   History – Auxiliary Sciences
D   History and Topography (except America)
E–F   America
G   Geography – Anthropology
H   Social Sciences – Sociology
J   Political Sciences
K   Law
L   Education
M   Music
N   Fine Arts
P   Language and Literature
Q   Science
R   Medicine
S   Agriculture – Plant and Animal Industry
T   Technology
U   Military Science
V   Naval Science
Z   Bibliography and Library Science

Within these large groupings, further letters and numbers give the subdivisions. I select one group to show how this is done.

N   Fine Arts

N   General
        8700–9084

NA   Architecture
        4600–6113   Religious architecture
        7100–7625   Domestic architecture.

NB   Sculpture and related arts

NC   Graphic Arts in general. Drawing and design. Illustration.
        1300–1765 Caricature. Pictorial humour and satire.

ND   Painting
        1700–2399   Water-colour painting.
        2890–3416   Illuminating of manuscripts and books.

NE   Engraving. Prints
        1000–1325   Wood engraving. Xylography. Japanese prints.
        1400–1775   Metal engraving. Colour prints.
        1940–2225   Etching. Dry point.
        2250–2539   Lithography

NK   Art applied to industry. Decoration and ornament.
        1700–3505   Interior decoration. Home decoration.
        3700–4695   Ceramics. Pottery.
        5000–6050   Enamel. Glass. Stained glass. Glyptic arts.

This is one example. Further information for other groups and for further subdivisions within this group may be found in *Outline of the Library of Congress Classification*.

Familiarity with these methods of placing books will enable students to go straight to what seems the most relevant section for their purpose. But to begin a research project here, at the open shelves, is inadequate and may prove misleading. Certain books may be out on loan; others may be held in stock in the basement. Then again, the physical grouping of books on a shelf may not correspond to the complexities of the subject. Even a simple case will demonstrate the point. Suppose one were writing a paper on the Greek civilization of the Classical era. One might start looking at the Ancient History shelves, and discover certain relevant volumes there. But an important work like Ehrenberg's *The Greek State* might be shelved under Political Science; Richter's *Greek Sculptors and Sculpture* under

Fine Arts; and Kitto's *Greek Tragedy* under Literature. It is clearly impossible to take in all the books relevant to a theme, scattered as they are around the library, merely by looking at the open shelves. The only way to make sense of the situation is by going back to the catalogue.

The Catalogue

The catalogue is the logical place to begin one's research. It is a register of all the books in the library. There are different methods of cataloguing the books and students will need to spend a little time familiarizing themselves with the one used by their own library.

A common method is to classify each book by author, title and subject. There are, however, several cards in the index for each book: those which identify a book by the author's name; those which list it under its title; and those which list it under one or more subject headings (such as Italian Renaissance or Shakespeare). In each case the information is entered on a 5 × 3 in. card (see Fig. 1).

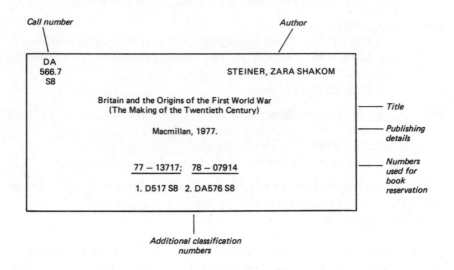

FIG. 1. Card index card.

From the researcher's point of view, there are three items of primary importance on this card: the author, title, and call number. To these may be added the date of publication, an important factor in assessing the worth of the book. The cards for each entry of the book are identical, except that those which list it under its title or subject have this additional heading typed above the author's name.

The subject cards are of obvious value to the researcher. If one is beginning an investigation from the start — that is, with little to go on but the subject approach — one has to use a little ingenuity, and not be put off by drawing a few blanks. Thus Socialist Party may yield nothing, but Political Parties will. It is as well to remember that the cross-referencing in the library may not be perfect, and it is always worthwhile to try under several subject headings. Thus I would investigate Machiavelli under Machiavelli; Italian Literature; Italian Renaissance; Italian History; Political Science. One might turn up several cards not duplicated under other subject headings. The more complex a subject, the more likely one is to need various and ingenious assaults upon the card index. One may obtain some idea of how various book titles may be listed under subjects, by taking a few examples where one knows the author and title, and looking up the card index to see what alternative listings they appear under.

But perhaps this method is not the one used. The card index may list only author and title and there may be additional methods to track down the books by subject. One such method, of great help to the researcher, is to have a separate small subject catalogue, which, instead of listing specific titles, gives the number classification under which to look in a separate classified catalogue. This classified catalogue lists all books in numerical/ alphabetical order of their Dewey Decimal/Library of Congress classification. Having determined the relevant number of one's own subject interest, it it as easy to check the titles under that classification as to run one's eye along the shelves. The big difference is that in the classified catalogue they are all there, whereas on the shelves many are missing, because they have been borrowed or are shelved elsewhere. The classified catalogue has further advantages. One can see at a glance such important details as publication date without actually handling the volume. Moreover, the classified catalogue has a cross-referencing facility to books, which because their subject matter may have other relevancies, have been shelved under another classification. An example will make this clear. For the specimen paper on Nazi Propaganda, the student went first to the Subject Index for National Socialist Party: Germany: History, and was thus directed to the Classified Catalogue DD253.2–253.8. (This particular library used the Library of Congress Classification.) Under these numbers a variety of relevant titles emerged, but so did others; for example, *Film Propaganda* classified as DK226.3 and *Propaganda and the German Cinema*, classified as PN3266.5. Each of these works was listed under the original classification number in square brackets. The usefulness of this classified system for obtaining a clear view of all relevant books held by that particular library, wherever shelved, needs no labouring.

Students may also need to familiarize themselves with other means of cataloguing beside the card index. As stocks of books increase and space becomes more limited, libraries increasingly turn to new forms of technology. One such method is the use of microforms. Some record all recent acquisitions on microfiches; others have transferred their whole catalogue to microfiches, or are in process of doing so. Since each microfiche can hold a very large number of titles, there is an obvious saving of space for the library. For the library users also, once they have mastered the techniques of scanning the microfiche, there is a great saving of effort.

The microfiches are contained in a binder, and each covers a portion of the alphabet, for the combined author and title catalogue, or a portion of the Numerical/Alphabetical classification, for the Classified Catalogue. The entry for each book contains essentially the same information as the card, but reduced to a very tiny form, which can be brought up to full size by the microfiche reader. To find the entry required it is necessary to place the microfiche on the plate of the microfiche reader in the correct position. The machine itself will have instructions for this placing, and for switching on and focusing. With a little practice, it is quick and easy to find the entry required. The machine is equipped with a grid (as in Fig. 2), each

A1	A2	A3	A4	A5	A6	A7	A8	A9	A10	A11	A12	A13	A14	A15	A16	A17	A18
B1	B2	B3	B4	B5	B6	B7	B8	B9	B10	B11	B12	B13	B14	B15	B16	B17	B18
C1	C2	C3	C4	C5	C6	C7	C8	C9	C10	C11	C12	C13	C14	C15	C16	C17	C18
D1	D2	D3	D4	D5	D6	D7	D8	D9	D10	D11	D12	D13	D14	D15	D16	D17	D18
E1	E2	E3	E4	E5	E6	E7	E8	E9	E10	E11	E12	E13	E14	E15	E16	E17	E18
F1	F2	F3	F4	F5	F6	F7	F8	F9	F10	F11	F12	F13	F14	F15	F16	F17	F18
G1	G2	G3	G4	G5	G6	G7	G8	G9	G10	G11	G12	G13	G14	G15	G16	G17	G18
H1	H2	H3	H4	H5	H6	H7	H8	H9	H10	H11	H12	H13	H14	H15	H16	H17	H18
I1	I2	I3	I4	I5	I6	I7	I8	I9	I10	I11	I12	I13	I14	I15	I16	I17	I18
J1	J2	J3	J4	J5	J6	J7	J8	J9	J10	J11	J12	J13	J14	J15	J16	J17	J18
K1	K2	K3	K4	K5	K6	K7	K8	K9	K10	K11	K12	K13	K14	K15	K16	K17	K18
L1	L2	L3	L4	L5	L6	L7	L8	L9	L10	L11	L12	L13	L14	L15	L16	L17	L18
M1	M2	M3	M4	M5	M6	M7	M8	M9	M10	M11	M12	M13	M14	M15	M16	M17	M18
N1	N2	N3	N4	N5	N6	N7	N8	N9	N10	N11	N12	N13	N14	N15	N16	N17	N18
O1	O2	O3	O4	O5	O6	O7	O8	O9	O10	O11	O12	O13	O14	O15	O16	O17	IND
P1	P2	P3	P4	P5	P6	P7	P8	P9	P10	P11	P12	P13	P14	P15	P16	P17	IND

Index

FIG. 2. Microfiche grid.

letter/number combination giving guidance as to where the particular information is located on the microfiche. By moving a pointer to the relevant square, the reader can quickly find the author or title required. The two squares on the bottom right of the grid, marked IND, should be located first, as they provide the index for location of information on that microfiche. Thus, if the author or title one wants is located at K8, one moves the pointer to that square. Once one becomes familiar with them, the microfiches will be found easier and quicker to read than a card index, especially as one can deal with a large bibliography from one location.

In many libraries both the card index and the microfiche have been superseded by the central computer database with a number of terminals. The student will find that the screen of the computer terminal gives clear instructions as to what needs to be typed in to secure the required information. One may search for a book by title; by author; by call number; by subject or by key word. Call number or subject searches will enable one to browse through the chosen category, by typing the appropriate instructions for that particular system to move forwards or backwards. Since the system used varies from library to library, the student is advised to read carefully the leaflets provided by that particular library which explain its own system, or to follow the on-screen display. Information in the entry is shorter than that on a catalogue card, but contains all that is essential to one's purpose.

Sample Computer Entry

GANNON, Franklin Reid: *British Press in Germany 1936–39.*
Call number: DD256.5 G278 1971.

It will be noted that the publication date is included.

As with the microfiche catalogue, the advantages of being able to carry out a rapid bibliography search from one location are obvious. The disadvantage of both systems is that at busy times there are often insufficient machines for the number of users, and each may be in use by one person for quite a long time.

In many libraries a combination of systems is used, with earlier works on a card index and later ones on computer database. Sometimes a microfiche catalogue is available as a back-up to the computer database. It is therefore advisable to be familiar with all the systems.

The catalogue, then, whatever form it takes, offers the major access to the books in the library. The investigation cannot end there, however, for two reasons. First, the catalogue refers only to books stocked in that library. Second, it will give very limited guidance to the periodical section.

The Periodical Section

The periodical section is, in some ways, the researcher's happy hunting ground. It is authoritative because it contains the work of specialist writers in specialist fields. It is often easier to publish a book, than an article in major journals. Then, it offers information which may be simply unavailable in book form, anywhere. It is principally a matter of time lag. A book takes a long time to write and a longer time to publish. Once published, it may retain its position of ever-diminishing authority for many years. But a reputable journal may contain fresh and important facts that are months, weeks, perhaps even days, old. No book can compare with this authority. The periodical section offers the researcher the prize of being as up-to-date on the subject as it is humanly possible to be.

How is information about these articles to be gleaned? The articles are not listed in the card index. Only the journal or newspaper would be listed, probably in a special catalogue within the periodical section. This special catalogue will guide one to the periodicals actually held by the library, current numbers of which can be investigated on the shelves. The student should browse around the open shelves of current periodicals which will give some idea of the astounding wealth of specialist journals. Bound or boxed collections of past numbers will also be available, probably shelved in another part of the library, or, for reasons of space, transferred to microfilm. The library staff are always happy to explain how to use microfilm machines. Familiarity with them is becoming increasingly necessary for research. Recent annual compilations of newspapers such as *The Times* and *The Sunday Times* are also now available as CD ROMs and these may be available in the library. The library staff will be able to help with information on what is available, and how to acquire access to it.

When the journals or newspapers relevant to the topic have been discovered, however, the student is still a long way from finding the particular articles needed, and for this must turn to the Bibliography section.

The Bibliography Section

The Bibliography section of the library provides students with a guide to information on their subjects more comprehensive than that readily discoverable from the catalogue. As its name implies, it is concerned with providing information about what books or articles have appeared on any given subject, whether stocked by that library or not.

In the Bibliography section will be found works giving classified lists of periodicals, such as *Ulrich's Periodicals Directory, Guide to Current British Journals* or *Willings Press Guide*. These will lead the student to relevant periodicals. Once located, they then have to be analysed. Such analysis is assisted by the fact that virtually all reputable journals publish an annual index. The major newspapers also produce comprehensive indexes. The Times group publishes an index, which includes not only *The Times*, but also *The Times Literary Supplement, The Times Educational Supplement*, and *The Times Higher Education Supplement*. There is also an index to the *Financial Times*. Major libraries may well have the indexes to foreign newspapers such as *The New York Times, Wall Street Journal* or *Le Monde*.

These indexes are of value if students know the journals in which articles on their subjects are likely to have appeared, or if they know that it will have been covered in the press. If they are merely looking to see what has been written, they will need further help. This is readily obtainable from the many publications devoted to the listing of periodical literature. These range from the general to the highly particularized and specialist. It is possible to list only some here.

The most comprehensive of the general works is *The Reader's Guide to Periodical Literature*. It calls itself 'a cumulative author subject index to periodicals of general interest published in the United States'. This gives some idea of its coverage. A list of the close to two hundred magazines for which articles are listed is printed in the front. It is published twice a month for about half the year, and otherwise monthly. It is cumulative. Students will therefore find the entries for the current year by their month, but the numbers for previous years reclassified into two yearly volumes. Necessarily, entries are brief and use a number of abbreviations which make the book appear difficult. At the front of each volume a sample abbreviated entry is given with full explanation below. Careful reading of this will soon enable students to follow the method used. Once they have mastered *The Reader's Guide*, they have mastered the system used for many other Guides. Entries are listed alphabetically under author, subject and sometimes title.

To illustrate how the system works: if one is studying the origins of the Social Democratic Party/Alliance, one will find entries under Political Parties: Great Britain. I take one at random.

Sample Entry

Left, right and rising centre. C. Kennedy, il. *Maclean's* 94:35 S 28 '81.

This means that an illustrated article, entitled 'Left, right and rising centre', by C. Kennedy, will be found in volume 94 of *Maclean's*, page 35, in the issue of 28 September 1981. It should be noted that a list of the abbreviations used for many journal names appears at the front of the Guide. Another important guide is *The Social Sciences Index*, which lists articles from about 300 English language periodicals, of which about 40 are British. It has a more restricted coverage, as its name implies, and is laid out on much the same lines as *The Reader's Guide*, again with subject and author entries. Older works, mostly of the last century, since its coverage goes only to 1906, can be found in *Poole's Guide to Periodical Literature*.

Besides these works concerned with periodicals and wide coverage, there are many specialist subject indexes published, listing books as well as articles. Thus for English Language and Literature, students will find the *Annual Bibliography of English Language and Literature*, published by Modern Humanities Research Association. It contains books, periodical articles, theses and book reviews, listed under subject and author. The volumes are cross-referenced so that an entry for a review will include details of the original entry for the book reviewed.

Sample Entry for the 1981 volume

HAYMAN, Ronald. *British Theatre since 1955: a reassessment.* (Bibl. 1979, 9152) Rev. by Eric Salmon in QQ (88) 137–44 (review article).

This means that the book was originally listed in the 1979 volume, item 9152, and that a review of it by Eric Salmon, as part of a review article, appears in *Queen's Quarterly*, volume 88, pages 137–144.

For the Social Sciences, as well as the *Social Sciences Index*, already mentioned for periodicals, students might turn to the *London Bibliography of Social Sciences*, which lists not only books and articles, but also pamphlets and periodicals. Thus for the Social Democratic Party it lists policy document pamphlets, and also *The New Democrat*, a monthly journal. A student of education might turn to *Education Index*, an American publication listing some British periodicals, or *British Education Index*.

It is possibe to give only a few examples here, but for the special index devoted to their own subject students are advised to turn to more general bibliographic works. In this context I would mention first the works of wide coverage. There is *A World Bibliography of Bibliographies* by Theodore Besterman. The Fourth and Final edition came out in 1965–6, but a decennial supplement based on the same principles has been compiled for 1964–74. Then there is *World Bibliographical Series* edited by Robert L. Collinson. These will lead students to specialist works in their own fields. Another invaluable work is *The Walford Guide to Reference Material*, which first appeared in 1959, but has been updated. It is in three volumes: Volume 1, Science and Technology, 1993; Volume II, Social and Historical Sciences, Philosophy and Religion, 1982; Volume III, Generalia, Language and Literature, the Arts, 1986. This work aims to provide a signpost to reference books and bibliographies published mainly in recent years. Bibliographies are listed under each subject. For example, under History, the *Annual Bulletin of Historical Literature*, published by the

Historical Association is listed. *The Walford Guide* is very wide in its coverage and, where appropriate, includes short quotations from reviews of works it cites. There is also *Walford's Concise Guide to Reference Material*, 1992.

Again, as with other aspects of the library, bibliographical searches are being revolutionised by the use of CD ROMs. These can provide an enormous database for articles in learned journals on a particular field, for theses titles and theses abstracts in Great Britain, North America and some European countries. Libraries with a well-equipped CD ROM section may be able to provide a CD ROM listing of all books in print from U.K. publishers, for example Bookbank. The material available is constantly being increased. As I write this *The Times Educational Supplement* has just produced *Bookfind* listing and reviewing 500,000 titles (1994). The library staff will have information as to which CD ROMs are available in their particular library.

Using these methods the student should be able to track down the appropriate bibliography. The value of this is that relevant books and periodicals not on the library shelves can be identified. They can then be ordered from another library through the Inter-library Loan system, or the researcher may pursue them to another library.

In this context it is worth noting that for every region of Britain there is a copyright library, that is one entitled to a copy of every book published in the United Kingdom. These copyright libraries are, for England, the British Library (London), the Cambridge University Library, the Bodleian Library (Oxford); for Scotland, the National Library of Scotland (Edinburgh); for Wales, the National Library of Wales (Aberystwyth); and for Ireland, Trinity College Library (Dublin). For newspapers, other than those in their own library, students should be aware of the existence of the British Library Newspaper Library, Colindale Avenue, London. There are also many large reference libraries and specialist libraries in Britain. The *ASLIB Directory* referred to on page 21 gives information on all specialist libraries.

The bibliographical works cited above, as well as the information gained on specialist libraries, are all part of a larger axiom: that researchers should not believe that the sum of human knowledge, relevant to their investigation, is confined to what is under their noses.

CHAPTER 2

Preparing a Bibliography

The first objective of the researcher is the preparation of as full a preliminary bibliography as practicable. The range of this bibliography will to some extent be determined by the requirements of the particular research paper. The types of research paper the student will be called upon to write will have a wide range. At one end of the scale a student's first assignment in this field may be a term paper, which is in essence no more than an extended essay relying on the two or three books which the library has available on the topic. At the other end may be a more ambitious venture that can fairly claim to be regarded as a minor contribution to original scholarship. Equally, students in specialized fields will concentrate their attention more particularly on some of the sources I have to consider, e.g. the Art students with visual material. To ensure that the needs of all these students are covered, I have given consideration here to all possible sources of information for even the most ambitious research project. Since I feel that even if one does not pursue the research programme with the utmost rigour, it is essential to know that it exists, I have in this chapter concentrated on the diversity and challenge of the research problem. Students whose assignments are more limited should not take fright at this, but, with the aid of their instructors, select the more readily available sources of information which will serve their needs.

To begin with, the distinction must be made between *primary* and *secondary* sources. Primary materials are first-hand accounts, reflections and statements. They are not based on other written works. They are in their original form, without having been arranged or interpreted by anyone else. Official documents, diaries and letters are the best examples of primary sources; but, generally, any sources which can be regarded as the researcher's raw material are primary. Secondary sources — by far the larger group — discuss primary sources. They consist of works which select, edit and interpret this raw material. A thoroughly integrated and well-grounded paper should draw if possible on both types of source. A historian is required to study, let us say, the letters of the Venetian Ambassador in conjunction with a general dissertation on Renaissance diplomacy. Students of art and literature must acquaint themselves with

19

the basic products of the artist and writer before going on to consider the discussions conducted by the appropriate critics. Even students of Dewey's educational theories must occasionally plunge into the thicket of Dewey's prose. All this is obvious enough; but even the most experienced scholars sometimes fall into the pitfall of considering what Professor X said about Z — to the exclusion of what Z actually said. However learned and brilliant the discussion by subsequent authorities, one must maintain contact with the material they are discussing. Apart from the need to draw some conclusions of one's own, it is here in the primary sources that little nuggets of information may be found that have been overlooked by other researchers, for one reason or another. It is such nuggets which may give distinction to one's own work.

Bearing in mind this distinction, between primary and secondary sources, the student must first make out a list of all the available sources that may bear upon the chosen field of study. The process of evaluation, selection, reading and note-taking will come later. But this process should not be begun without a full, if rapid, survey of the sources.

These are of much greater diversity than is often realized, or exploited. The obvious sources, books and journals, I have already discussed in the previous chapter, together with the bibliographical guidance to them. But there are numerous other sources, published and unpublished, that may bear investigation.

Published Sources

Many institutions issue their own printed material. The most obvious ones which spring to mind are government departments. Her Majesty's Stationery Office (HMSO) issues free about seventy sectional lists offering guidance to what is available. In their own words: 'The aim of the series of catalogues known as Sectional Lists is to show titles of HMSO publications currently in print. Most deal with publications prepared by particular government departments.' A few of the sectional lists deal with particular subjects: for example, No. 60, *Histories of the First and Second World Wars and Peacetime Series*; or No. 69, *Overseas Affairs*.

Not all British government publications are from HMSO, however. Some departments produce their own material. Further information on this may be obtained from *British Official Publications* by J. E. Pemberton, or *Official Publications* by David Butcher.

Another major institution whose publications need to be considered is the United Nations. It issues the *United Nations Library Monthly Bibliography*: I. *Books, Official Documents, Serials*; II. *Selected Articles*. The Library of the United Nations Information Centre (14-15 Stratford Place, London W.1) would be able to supply information on United Nations publications.

These are the most obvious sources of official publications, but many more are available. Further information on those which may be relevant to the student's own particular topic should be sought in the Bibliography section of the Library. There are two especially useful guides. One is the two-volume *ASLIB Directory*. Volume One is *Information Sources in Science, Technology and Commerce*, Volume Two *Information Sources in Medicine, the Social Sciences and the Humanities*. These volumes are regularly updated. They provide a list of addresses of information sources on all manner of subjects, giving information and publications from, for example, government departments, industry, and societies. The other useful bibliographical source is the three-volume *Walford Guide to Reference Material*, already discussed in the previous chapter.

From these sources students will find what is relevant to their own subjects. Most libraries have a large stock of such material, but it will not normally be listed in the general catalogue. Students may find that in their own particular library it occupies a separate section with its own catalogue. Consultation of the library layout plan, or with the librarian, will help them track down what is already there, and the guides will show them how to procure access to what is not. The important thing is to be alive to the possibilities of its existence, and to explore them.

The same holds true for other material of an ephemeral nature which needs to be taken into consideration. There are, for example, current, non-indexed newspapers; catalogues to an art exhibition; press handouts, as of a candidate's speech in an election; pamphlets, news-sheets, and advertisements of all kinds, including handouts from industrial firms. Again, the printed word does not account for all published sources. Records of the spoken word extend back to Tennyson and Browning; the film is not much younger; the camera came of age during the American Civil War, but for many years previously photographs had recorded the social and natural scene. To these may now be added tape recordings, for example, of radio programmes, and video recordings of television programmes. The various albums, film-reels and recordings — whether restricted now to museum collection, or currently available in commercial form — represent a giant supplement to the printed and published sources of the past century.

Unpublished Sources

Writings which have not been made available to the general public are numerous. Diaries, letters, memoranda, rough drafts of writings published later, accounts, church registry entries, can be of enormous importance. The tendency is naturally for the most important of these records to gravitate towards the major libraries. Others remain to be sought out in the archives, national and local, all over the country; and yet more repose in private hands. Guidance as to what may be available is provided by *Guide to the Contents of the Public Record Office*, issued in three volumes by HMSO, and Sectional List No. 24, British National Archives. The *Walford Guide* provides a National Index to Parish Registers.

Initiative allied to luck can unearth the most astonishing finds even now —and I am not referring to an exceptional field like archaeology. It is not so very long since Dr. Leslie Hotson discovered, in a quite straighforward visit to the Public Record Office, the official record of the inquest on Marlowe's death by violence. Even more recently, Byron's official biographer has found a hitherto unknown work by the poet, amongst some miscellaneous papers in the possession of his publishers, John Murray. A steady stream of less dramatic discoveries continues to reach the public; for example, the letters and diaries of those serving in the two World Wars. And this is merely the tip of the iceberg. To be sure, the relevance of such material is more obvious in the fields of literature and history than in others. But in all areas of human endeavour there is a chance that a letter, an entry in a autograph album, a draft remains behind to supplement or even modify our ideas, based on published sources, of the matter. Whether this material is in public or private hands, it is the business of researchers to bring it to light if they can.

What is true of the printed word remains true of non-printed products. The various semi-permanent forms that human activity takes — architecture, technology, art — are frequently, of their essence, unique. An example is old gravestones. But surely such remains can be photographed, and then published in book form? Certainly, but it would be naive to suppose that such publications constitute any more than a limited and often misleading selection of the material to hand, influenced as they are by fashion, chance, and lack of knowledge. Art history is a good case in point. We know that Dürer was a great artist; we are only now coming to realize the greatness of Witz. The work of one has been much publicized for many years; of the other, not. The writer of one of the volumes in the Pelican History of Art* confessed that scarcely a week passed without the emergence of some previously unknown painting that caused him to modify his view. My point is this: there exists a vast corpus of relics that simply have to be seen. It is inadequate to rely on the photographed and published selection of these relics. In such situations the attribute of a good researcher approximates to that of a good reporter — leg-work.

Finally, there remain human contacts: letters or conversations. A source does not require the accolade of a permanent form to make it acceptable. There is no reason at all why a researcher should not attempt to approach a

* Ellis Waterhouse, *Painting in Britain 1530–1790*. Harmondsworth, 1962, p. xv.

living politician, or writer, or artist, to consult him or her about some
aspect. If successful, the result may be a fascinating series of insights into
matters not adequately covered by the existing sources. It is not only the
famous who can add a more immediate and personal dimension to the
researcher's work. In the field of social history especially, the tape-
recorded interview with those who were personally involved can be of
great value. An oral account is, in its way, every bit as valuable as a written
record. If unsuccessful, then one will have tried. And the worst that can
happen is that one will be sent away with a flea in one's ear.

Recording the Bibliography

All these sources, published and unpublished, must be recorded before
one can make a reasonable selection and whittle them down to a working
bibliography. Since the details of each source used will be needed in a most
exact form for footnotes and bibliography, it is necessary that extreme care
should be exercised at this stage to ensure that they are full and correct.
The conventional method is to write the relevant information for each
source on a separate 5 × 3 in. card. In the top left-hand corner should be
written the Library Call Number and, if more than one library is being
used, a note as to which library the book is from. This will enable time to
be saved in subsequent book location. The rest of the card should contain
the bibliographical information. In addition, the student may well add a
light annotation, based on a quick impression of the work (which may have
been handled physically on the shelves). Thus, on a solid historical
textbook published in the 1950s, one might annotate: 'Looks a readable
survey — probably written too long ago for a final view — best read first'.
Of some brilliant but wayward-looking piece of Shakespearian interpretation one might comment: 'Check reviews'. These quick impressions can be
immensely useful later.

The point of restricting each card to one source, and one only, is that it
makes the later business of discarding and rearrrangement a matter of the
greatest ease. The longer the work, the greater the number of sources
considered, the more important it becomes to be in a position to arrange
the sources alphabetically (by author) for quick consultation. Anyone who
thinks this is a rather childish simplification should try the task of sorting
out a list of a hundred or so titles which have simply been entered, as they
come, in an ordinary notebook. It is not a labour one would wish to repeat.

The form for the bibliographical material varies according to the source
itself. There is no one absolutely standardized procedure accepted by all
authorities. Individual publishing houses often have their own in-house
style, for example, and some universities issue their own guidelines on the
presentation of theses. The student should adopt a system and maintain it
consistently. The one recommended here is in conformity with the

principles laid down in the *Modern Humanities Research Association Style Book* (3rd edition, 1981). For the United States the ultimate authority is the Modern Language Association of America's *The MLA Style Sheet*, and its recommendations, given in helpfully exhaustive detail and thus covering every eventuality, would also be generally acceptable in Britain.

The Forms of Bibliography Cards for Books

For all bibliography cards the author's last name is given first to facilitate the arrangement of the cards in alphabetical order for the final bibliography. The form which the information takes in the final version will be different for footnotes, from that of the final bibliography, as will be seen below (Chapter 5). The required information should be taken from the title page or, in the case of the date and edition, the next page.

Author or authors and title. Below the call number should be written the name of the author, last name first, followed by a comma, first name(s) or initials, followed by a comma; and the name of the book, underlined.

Examples

Norman, Charles, *The Muses' Darling: Christopher Marlowe.*
Lovejoy, A. O., *The Great Chain of Being.*

It should be noted that in the first title a colon had to be supplied, since publishers set out, rather than punctuate, their titles.

Where there is more than one author, the first author should be listed last name first, as for a single author, followed by a comma, and the subsequent author(s) in normal order, separated by commas.

Example

McLuhan, Marshall, and Quentin Fiore, *The Medium is the Massage.*

If there are more than three authors, it is the practice to put *et al.* or 'and others' after the name of the first author.

Example

Parker, Geoffrey, and others, *The Thirty Years War.*

If the work of an author is translated or edited by someone else, this additional information should be given after the author's name and the title of the work.

Example

Castiglione, Baldesar, *The Book of the Courtier*, trans. Charles S. Singleton, ed. Edgar de N. Mayhew.

There may, however, be no author but only an editor or compiler. In this case, list the work by its title followed by a comma and the name of the editor.

Example
> *The Nazi Years: a Documentary History*, edited by Joachim Remak.

If the work is produced by a public body, list it by its title and include the other information with the publishing details.

Example
> *Case Studies in multicultural education: a series of documentary films
> — Discussion leader's notes* (British Broadcasting Corporation,
> London, 1981).

The publishing details. The number of the edition used, if it is not the first, is given next in Arabic numerals, e.g. 2nd ed., also any further information such as 'revised and enlarged'. Information where relevant should also be given as to the number of volumes.

The place of publication followed by a comma, followed by the date of publication, is written below the title and the edition details, if any. Figure 3 shows the layout of a complete card, giving these publishing details, and

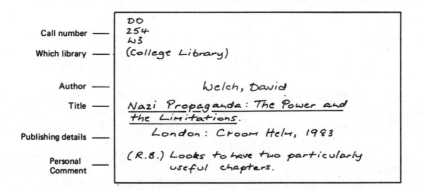

FIG. 3. Specimen bibliography card.

also the researcher's personal comment, on the last line. Some organizations like to have details of the actual publisher, but this is now not standard practice and is not recommended by either of the authorities cited above. Rather, the tendency is to simplify bibliographical details.

The Forms of Bibliography Cards for Articles

The cards for magazine and newspaper articles, articles from general collections, book reviews, etc., are similar to the ones for books, but the form for the titles varies, and the publication details are necessarily somewhat different.

Thus the author(s), translator, etc., details will be given in the same form as for a book. The title of the article, however, is enclosed in single quotation marks, and followed by a comma, unless the title ends in a question mark or exclamation mark. If the article appears in a book, the title will be followed by 'in', and the name of the book, underlined, followed by publication details, as set out above for books.

Example

> Kershaw, Ian, 'How Effective was Nazi Propaganda?' in *Nazi Propaganda*, edited by David Welch (London, 1983), pp. 180–221.

If the article appears in a journal or newspaper, the title will be followed by the name of the journal or newspaper, underlined, followed by a comma and publication details. These latter are clearly different from those given for a book. What is now required is a means of identifying the particular issue. Thus, for a journal, the volume number is given, in Arabic numerals, followed by the year of publication, and sometimes also the month or season, of publication, in parentheses, followed by a comma and the numbers of pages.

Example

> Arnott, Peter, 'Some Costume Conventions in Greek Tragedy', *Essays in Theatre*, Vol. 2, No. 1 (November 1983), pp. 3–18.

It should be noted that the comma comes after, not before, the parentheses. In the case of newspapers and weekly or monthly magazines, the volume number may be omitted and the complete date given, separated by commas, and not in parentheses.

Example

> Ezra, Derek, 'What Future now for Coal?', *The Observer,* 17 February 1985, p. 10.

There may be no author for the article and, if so, this fact should be noted where possible. For example, an editorial should have the word 'editorial' in parentheses after the title and before the comma, e.g. 'New and Wrong Terms' (editorial). An anonymous review, or unsigned article, should have this fact noted in the same way.

Bibliography Cards for Other Material

Unpublished sources should also be noted in the bibliography by whatever method is appropriate. For example, documents, unpublished theses, etc., may be identified by the author, if there is one, and location; letters and interviews by the name of the person concerned and the date; a lecture by the lecturer, the title of the lecture in quotation marks, as for the title of an article, and the place and date of delivery. A similar entry would also be made for a television or radio broadcast, except that the place of delivery would be replaced by the channel, or station. Visual material should also be identified by an entry giving its exact location, as: inscription on the tomb of Lord Chief Justice Tanfield, St. John Baptist Church, Burford, Oxfordshire.

Evaluating the Bibliography

Now comes the operation of reducing the initial bibliography to a smaller, working bibliography. I shall treat this as an entirely separate phase from the preceding one; but in practice there may be an overlap. It may take, for example, some time to elicit replies to correspondence enquiries. In the interim the student may as well get on with the job of evaluating the sources already listed. It is, however, always helpful to think of the research work as a series of orderly, planned phases. Life will contribute its own quota of disorderly, unplannable elements — there is no need to add to them unduly.

I assume, then, that everything within reason has been done to prepare a full list of sources. We now consider this bibliography. It may be quite a small one — on certain very contemporary topics a working bibliography is, quite simply, all that one can find out. In such cases there is no problem. But usually the difficulty is one of restriction.

What makes a source acceptable, or more precisely, preferable? Of the infinite variety of factors that bear upon this matter, I single out two for special mention: the date of publication, and the standing of the author.

The date can very easily be weighed. It is, of course, generally true to say that the more modern a book is, the better. One can reasonably assume a second or later edition of a work to be corrected and revised. Again, the writer may be limited, but like all of us is a beneficiary of progress. Knowledge accumulates. So modernity counts; but this is much more true of some areas than others. Thus a book on nuclear submarines, published in 1958, is of very limited value. One may assume it to contain an accurate view of submarines up till 1958; but so much has occurred since then that the book is bound to be outdated. In this field nothing less that the latest edition of *Jane's Fighting Ships* would suffice. On the other hand, for a thorough and well-documented history of the English Civil Wars, the historian still turns to S. R. Gardiner's *History of the Commonwealth and Protectorate*, the first volume of which was published in 1903. I suggest that one should select from new and the old in the matter of dates. One should always have a representative of the very latest publications, and indeed aim at a preponderance of fairly recent works. But there is usually a case for including a well-written work that contains a readable epitome of the orthodox view a generation ago. What in practice one has to do is to cut out a mass of the dead wood that accumulates in libraries over the years.

The standing of the author is a far more complex issue. Often one simply does not know, and cannot know. Reputation is an elusive aura. Just how good is Professor X? I can only suggest certain pointers here that the student can look for. The book may have gone through several editions. The testimony of the publisher is, to put it mildly, untrustworthy; but, if the dust-jacket refers to Professor X's 'standard' work, and the book has run through several editions, there is a fair chance that the publisher's claims may not be a league away from the truth. Somebody must have bought it. Often enough a dust-jacket (or title-page) will make a bibliographical reference to the background and qualifications of the author, or these can be discovered from *Who's Who*, and here again readers can judge for themselves (or, possibly, draw certain inferences from the lack of satisfactory data). Favourable reviews of a previous edition may be cited on the dust-jacket. Additionally, the work may be cited in a published bibliography—for example, at the end of an article on the subject in a good encyclopedia.

All this, however, can indicate only very approximately the value of a work. The nearest approach to the truth must be obtained from the judgement of one's peers. The reviews are crucial, and ought to be studied. It is true that the same difficulties arise with the standards of reviewing, as of writing. Critics can be incompetent, biased and unfair. But a jury of sorts exists; a consensus exists. Apart from the specialist scholarly journals, from which a considered review of a specialist work can be expected, one can look with confidence to certain newspapers and periodicals of established reputation and high standards. A forum of informed contemporary criticism is provided by, for example, *The Times, The Times Literary Supplement, The Sunday Times, The Observer, Spectator, New Statesman and Society* and *London Review of Books*. These are British publications, but an American publication of high repute, held by many university libraries, is *The New York Review of Books*. The list could be extended, but these provide a reliable cross-section likely to be readily available in the library.

Useful guidance to reviews is provided by certain specialist works. The most important and comprehensive of these is the *Book Review Digest*, published monthly with annual cumulation. This contains shortened reviews from selected periodicals, a list of which appears at the beginning of the Guide. Usually not more than three reviews are actually quoted, but others are cited so that they may be readily found. Another comprehensive work is the *Book Review Index*. It is published bi-monthly, with annual cumulation, and a master cumulation for the decade 1969–79. More than 400 journals are indexed and references given to books that have been reviewed only once, as well as those reviewed more frequently. Reviews are not quoted, but the citations will readily lead the reader to the full review. Another more specialized work is *An Index to Book Reviews in the Humanities*. This work also cites, but does not quote, reviews from many learned journals.

With the aid of such works as these the student may readily track down the reviews. True, one can hardly consult them all. But one should get into the habit of checking one or two reviews, especially when a rather extreme thesis seems to be propounded.

And this leads me to my next point in this discussion of the evaluation problem. Most writers have a 'thesis' — a point of view which they seek to advance. Put more bluntly, they have an axe to grind. This is well enough; impartiality is an impossible ideal, and one does well to be sceptical of those who profess it. But it is necessary to bear in mind the author's predispositions. Is he or she an old-guard Freudian, or a revisionist, or does he or she regard psychoanalysis as finished? Is the author a Marxist, or merely Left-of-Centre; young or old; (on matters affecting the social activity of a given country) a native, or a foreigner? If it is practicable, one ought to set authorities at each other's throat in one's own work. The great failing in assessing one's sources is to fall under the spell of one powerfully written work. Let the opposition speak too.

There are many instances where an individual has staked a reputation or career on a particular point of view. Churchill's commitment to anti-appeasement springs immediately to mind. In his *War Memoirs* he argues powerfully and convincingly that Britain was wrong in 1938. But not even from a Churchill should a researcher accept an account uncritically. Churchill violently opposed the Munich settlement at the time; his career was intimately bound up with its consequences. He is, therefore, an immensely formidable, but highly committed advocate. So one looks to the other side for a statement of the government's case. One would anticipate, and in fact correctly, that the official biographer of Neville Chamberlain (Keith Feiling), and his later biographer (Iain Mcleod), would provide such a statement. There are naturally other later historians not passionately committed to either view. An equally controversial issue, with persuasive and committed writers, was the Suez Crisis. Here one would need to set against Anthony Eden, who argues his own case powerfully in the first volume of his memoirs (*Full Circle*), *No End of a Lesson* by Anthony Nutting, who resigned over the issue and ruined his political career. A perhaps more notorious instance of purely academic argument is A. J. P. Taylor's view of the causes of the Second World War. This has stirred up so much controversy that it has even resulted in a book, devoted to A. J. P. Taylor and his critics. The lesson to be gained from these instances is that no authority is final. None.

Assessing one's authorities must remain one of the most difficult aspects of the research problem. All that one can do in the way of ferreting out information — from one's instructor, or the dust-jacket, or the reviews — is subject to the arbitrament of judgement. And the trouble with judgement, as A. E. Housman observed, is that if one has not got it, one never misses it. If Professor X is after all no good, some people will never find that out. But at least safety can be sought in numbers, and in a certain scepticism. Reliance on these allies will save a student from falling too easy a prey to Calvin Hoffman's view of Shakespeare, or a Marxist's view of Western society.

CHAPTER 3

Taking Notes

The labour of taking notes requires the utmost exactitude and discipline. Without a strict organization, the process can degenerate very easily into chaos. Supposing one approaches the matter carelessly — or naturally. One might simply jot down ideas, facts, opinions as they come, into a notebook, without reference to where they were obtained, or whether they are one's own ideas or those extracted from the writer. One would then be left, several books later, with a mass of unsortable, unverifiable material, some of which could not even be assigned to its original source. The physical difficulties of reshaping material which has been entered consecutively into a notebook are obvious enough; and the labour of rechecking a badly-taken note (what I mean by this term will be apparent later in the chapter) is almost too painful to contemplate. So the job has to be done well, first time; and for that two points must be established: the necessity for note-cards, and for a systematized mode of noting down information.

Note-Cards

First, the note-cards. They are the answer to the notebook problem. The best practice is to use 6 × 4 in. cards. This is because it is convenient to use (of the standard sizes) a different one from the 5 × 3 in. bibliography cards, to avoid confusion, and because there is more room for note-taking on the larger cards. (A very large handwriting might require an 8 × 5 in. size, but normally 6 × 4 in. is ample.) A single note is taken on each card; a note consisting of one idea.

What are the benefits of this system? They are two-fold. Note-cards can be rejected; and they can be rearranged. These are immense advantages; for we can say with certainty of all research, that too many notes will be taken, and in the wrong order. Researchers begin by taking notes of everything that they think might be useful. Some of the material will prove to be superseded by later material; some will prove to be, quite simply, not as useful or relevant as was first thought likely; some will have to be pruned, or excised in the interests of space. *Waste is inseparable from research.* But it is simplicity itself to reject unwanted notes from the sheaf

31

that has been accumulated. Re-arrangement is facilitated even more. There is no way of ensuring that one takes notes in the identical order to that in which they will appear in the finished work. Therefore, one has to shuffle the pack. This is very easy, if one has a pack, and not the refractory pages of a notebook, each page containing several notes of varying usefulness.

I labour the point, but it is worth labouring. And I add that all this applies with astronomically mounting force to longer projects. One might just manage to control one's material, old-style, if one is writing up a term paper on the basis of a single authoritative book. But for a long-term, ambitious piece of research, covering a variety of sources, the concept is ridiculous. Not to use note-cards is evidence of a horse-and-buggy mentality.

The System of Note-taking

What should go on to the note-cards? One idea only, certainly, else the advantages of atomization are lost. But the techniques of recording the idea must be rigorously applied. Essentially, each card contains three items of information: a descriptive label, or some identifying phrase; the main body of the note itself; and the reference to the source. A sample card is shown in Figure 4. That is the simplest form which a note-card could take.

Characterization in Shakespeare

"The modern conception of character has therefore been granted inappropriate to Shakespeare, and so presumably to his contemporaries."

Bradbrook, p. 54

FIG. 4. Simple specimen note-card.

There is a heading, relating the card to the theme the writer is pursuing; the note itself, a direct quotation; and the reference to its source. It should be noted that the source is identified as simply as possible. There is no need to copy out in full: M. C. Bradbrook, Themes and Conventions of Elizabethan Tragedy, p. 54. The student has already made a full note of all publication details in the bibliography. But if any *other* work by M. C.

Bradbrook is being used, the title will have to be identified, at least briefly. The note might then be written: Bradbrook, <u>Themes</u>, p. 54. The page number is a precise, but necessary narrowing down of the reference. It has to be possible for the researcher to check on the notes, *and for a future reader to check on the researcher*. The whole foundation of scholarship rests on full and accurate identification of the means whereby one has arrived at one's conclusions. Hence the need to record the details which will later be recorded in one's footnotes.

Precision is called for in writing out the main body of the note, a matter we have now to consider in greater detail. There are in fact three types of notes that one can take: a direct quotation, as in the example; a paraphrase or summary of the original passage; and the writer's own opinions. These must be rigidly distinguished.

Let us now consider the circumstances in which one chooses a direct quotation or a paraphrase. Why does one take the note originally? Because, obviously, one considers the point of sufficient importance. But it may be important for different reasons. The original writer may have made a classic, and succinct, statement of the position; it is so well expressed that the language cannot be improved on. Here a direct quotation is in order. Or the statement, even if badly expressed, may be so fundamental to the writer's position that it should be quoted in its entirety. Again, statements in which every word counts — as in a legal or philosophic context — should be noted exactly.

There are, however, many more instances in which it is quite unnecessary to retain the exact words of the original writer. Very often a whole chapter can be rendered down to a few succinct sentences. Large quantities of data can be summarized in a few generalizations. One paraphrases a passage for the importance of its *content*; one quotes it directly for the additional importance of its *mode of expression*.

In either case, the form is precise. An original quotation should be followed in all respects. If the text uses American or outmoded spelling, it should be copied scrupulously. An error or fatuity in the text should be copied, and followed with [*sic*] which means 'thus in the original'. If anything has been omitted from the passage copied, the fact should be indicated with ellipsis marks. Three spaced full stops, preceded by a space, are used for ellipsis within a sentence, thus (. . .); and three spaced full stops in addition to the final full stop, if the matter to be omitted comes at the end of the sentence. If a considerable amount is omitted, a line or more of verse, or a paragraph or more of prose, this fact should be indicated by a single line of spaced full stops. If words have to be inserted to make sense of a passage, they should be enclosed in square brackets [ ] to distinguish them from the parentheses ( ) that might occur naturally in the text quoted. Square brackets are an indication always of an editorial intervention of some kind: that is an interpolation by the writer of explanatory matter, or comment, into the text being dealt with. The complete quotation, with or without excisions or additions, should be enclosed in single quotation marks, and any quotations within it should be enclosed in double quotation marks, the writer making this change if necessary.

A paraphrase takes a precise form in that it is written down without quotation marks. This is not a verbal quibble. The researcher has to feel absolute confidence in the notes. If the quotation marks are present, that is proof that the quotation is an exact copy of the original; if quotation marks are not present, that is proof that the words are the researcher's own. It should be strongly emphasized here that the words must be genuinely the researcher's own, and show that the thought has been assimilated and not merely slightly reworded. A good plan is to read the passage through carefully, think about it a moment or two, then lay it aside and write the note without looking at the actual text, then check again to make sure that the original author has not been misrepresented. The positive and negative implications of the presence or absence of quotation marks are, then, far-reaching. But, it may be objected, surely students can tell their own words from someone else's anyway? No, they cannot. Notes taken a few weeks or months previously may have been, to all intents and purposes, written by an entirely different person. It is simply not possible to read one's own writing, after the lapse of some time, and distinguish with complete confidence in all cases between one's own words and another's. Without the apparatus I have outlined above, without the reliance on exact techniques, students will always face a twinge of doubt when they confront their notes, and come to write them up in their pages. They are then faced with unpleasing alternatives. Suppose their memory is at fault, they may advance their own paraphrase as an exact quotation — and thus blur or mar a statement where every word counts. Or they may do the reverse, and borrow another writer's exact words without acknowledgement, which in the scholarly context is just plain dishonest. Or they may avoid these pitfalls and look up the passage again — which is pure waste of time; they might just as well have got it right in the first place.

It should be emphasized at this point that in taking their notes students must guard themselves very carefully against the charge of plagiarism. The necessity of being certain whether one's own words or the author's are being used, and of avoiding paraphrase which is so close to the original as to amount to plagiarism, has already been mentioned. Even in summary, however, where the words are indubitably one's own, one must be careful to note the exact source of the information, since due acknowledgement will have to be made, in the paper, of ideas, theories or obscure facts. Failure to make this acknowledgement is just as much plagiarism as the borrowing of another author's exact words. One should therefore be extremely careful to note the page references. It is perhaps as well to mention here that it is a great convenience to mark on the note-card, where the break occurs, if a quotation extends across two pages. This may be done by inserting two parallel lines, thus //, where the page change occurs, or by inserting the number of the new page in parentheses, as in the following example: 'Ideas of tolerance came // to the West only after two or three centuries of literacy and visual Gutenberg culture.' Or 'Ideas of tolerance came (p. 303) to the West . . .'. This practice will be found useful if the writer later decides to use only part of the quotation.

So much for the vital distinction between direct quotation and paraphrase, and for the dangers of plagiarism. The third type of note, personal comment by the researcher, is an extremely valuable record of stray ideas that flash across the mind in the process of note-taking, and which can easily be lost if not quickly noted down; but they have to be labelled to avoid confusion. The same point applies as before. The intrusion of one's own ideas among those of Professor X may lead, months later, to the confident claim that the professor's ideas are one's own, or vice versa. Since one tends to assimilate ideas, the delusion is easy. I recommend, therefore, that all personal comment should be preceded by one's initials. Such a note-card looks amusingly like a fragment of Boswellian dialogue — but the techniques have dispelled any possibility of confusion.

One last point. It is convenient, and often useful, to number one's cards consecutively. This makes possible cross-reference in one's notes: as with an annotation, 'See 51 and 73'.

A more sophisticated version of a note, then, might look something like what is shown in Figure 5. The note-taker has entered in its original form a well-expressed statement. At the same time certain doubts as to the

Social Strata in Industry   89

"We come back to the basic distinction that, whereas the middle classes move forward by individual initiative, the workers gain their advances as a result of group activity."

Shanks, p. 61

(R.8.) Is this true today? Check on current surveys of m/class group activities, (Education? Professional organisations? Representation of Professions among M.P.s? Check Sociological Journals.)
(R.8.) See cards 120 - 124.

FIG. 5. Specimen note-card of greater complexity.

continuing truth of the observation have been jotted down, and a few pointers for future reference have been added. Later on the suggestion has been followed up (cards 120–126) and it has been found possible to add a cross-reference at the foot of the original card, No. 89.

Photocopying Material

Increasingly students find the convenience of photocopying at least some of the information used in preparation for writing their research papers. They may use a print-out facility with CD ROMs to copy blocks of text or illustrations. Photocopying or print-outs are particularly useful for such material as charts; tables of statistics; maps or illustrations. It can be valuable for the retention for future closer study of portions of a book, or article, particularly important to the student's theme. These sections may need to be looked at carefully later in the research, when more knowledge has been accumulated, and the student's viewpoint may have shifted. It is as useful to have them in a photocopy as to have the book itself; indeed, in some cases, as will be suggested below, it may be even more useful.

There are, however, certain dangers (apart from the expense involved!). Too much photocopying may consist in the mindless accumulation of piles of unassimilated pages. Without careful documentation at the time of the photocopying, later attribution of sources may be difficult. Finally the student may once again find the problem stated at the beginning of this chapter of the physical difficulties of shaping the material.

I will take these points one at a time. First, it is a good practice to ask oneself before photocopying: do I need to photocopy this material or can I summarize the main ideas on note-cards, so that it will be more handy for future reference? The same question can be applied to the number of pages photocopied, so as to reduce the material as far as possible. A rigorous application of these principles will ensure that the material is not unassimilated, since its relevance to the theme will be constantly checked. After it has been photocopied it may, of course, be gone through and underlined or highlighted to bring out the important points. Indeed, in this respect the photocopy is superior to a book. The writer may use it, in effect, as a notebook, and scribble comments in the margin with no fear of mistaking these words or ideas for those of the writer. This is a treatment that obviously cannot be applied to a library book, and that one would be loath to apply to a book of one's own, except possibly a very cheap and expendable paperback.

Secondly, the student should get into the habit of writing full details of the book or article from which the photocopied material came, on the first page, and of stapling the pages together at once, so that they do not become mixed up with other photocopied material. Thus attribution can be properly made in the research paper and the dangers of plagiarism avoided.

Lastly, it may be found that the use of a few note-cards, referring to the photocopied material, will help to overcome the physical problems of the need to shuffle the notes. For example, a note-card for each of the main ideas, with a reference 'see photocopy p.— for further details', will enable the material to be inserted easily in the correct place in the argument of the research paper.

By using these methods the student can gain all the advantages of photocopying without losing the advantages of note-cards.

And so the pile of cards accumulates. The more cards in the pile, the more manifestly efficient the whole procedure is; for the sheer bulk of the operation fractures a less orderly structure. The efficiency of the procedure rests on two principles: the atomization of knowledge, and the absolute reliance the researcher can place on the techniques of coding knowledge.

CHAPTER 4

Composing the Paper

The mass of data has now to be converted to a draft. We can usefully think of this operation as having three phases: making a skeleton outline, preparing an initial rough draft, and improving the rough draft.

Making a Skeleton Outline

This is the most intellectually exacting part of the whole process. Order must be imposed upon chaos, and it is at this precise point that the forces of chaos and order meet. Some two or three hours of uninterrupted thought should be set aside to consider the matter; it is not to be tackled in a stray half-hour; once the material has been set into a form, the mould will be hard to break and harder to alter. The writer has the task of reading, very rapidly, and very lightly, over the notes. Not much of the detail, of course, can be remembered at this stage. The aim is to impregnate the mind with as much as possible of the data. Only then can the material begin to be shaped.

Shape implies arrangement and rejection. The latter is hard. It is understandable that students should want to use a great deal of their notes. People feel a natural and human desire to demonstrate the full extent of their labours. But, as I have said before, waste is inseparable from research. Students must reconcile themselves to this, and be prepared ruthlessly to abandon large tracts of notes should they prove to be superfluous or unacceptable.

Such a decision can only be taken in the light of a constant brooding on the *purpose* of the project. Even now, at this late stage, the exact title may not be fixed. If it is, this title should be allowed to dominate the choice of material; if not, the mental energies of the writer should be directed towards crystallizing the title. At this stage, the problem is normally one of restriction. The writer has a full conspectus of the notes. The question must be asked: 'Can I carry out the project on the lines which I first intended? Or, with this mass of material, should I limit my scope?' Perhaps a historical resumé has to be compressed, so as to allow the major period to be properly studied. Perhaps some interesting and worthwhile side issues have to be abandoned. Perhaps a complex and controversial problem looks to be getting out of control; so the writer decides to play safe and concentrate only on those aspects of the matter that can be adequately handled. All these problems are intimately connected in a chain that extends from title to outline, from outline to selection of material.

I assume these problems to be provisionally settled, and turn to the details of the outline problem. This problem I define as *the search for internal form*. Every topic has a natural form, and it is the business of the writer to explore and clarify this form. I can best illustrate the point with some examples.

(a) The easiest of forms occurs within historic topics. The secret of history, as Churchill says, is chronology. So one has simply to begin at the beginning (whenever this point is judged to be) and carry on. There may be a secondary problem of judgement in dividing time into phases, but this is no great matter. Thus a general analysis of a historic phenomenon would break the subject down into Origins; Development; Results. The Munich Crisis can very reasonably be judged to start (as far as any historic problem can be so judged) from 1919, the date of the Treaty of Versailles. The period 1919–38 covers the origins of the Crisis, and can reasonably be subdivided into two phases: 1919–33 (the accession to power of Hitler) and 1933–8. As for the results, one would certainly have to consider its effect on the beginning of the War, in 1939, and perhaps take the question as far as 1940–1. After that the question becomes too speculative. So a likely outline for a paper on the 1938 Munich Crisis looks like this:

Part I: Origins (A) 1919–33, (B) 1933–8
Part II: The Crisis
Part III: The Aftermath 1938–40

We can add to this a brief Introduction, which states the main purpose and direction of the paper; and a Conclusion which returns to the purpose statement in the Introduction and reviews it in the light of the material examined.

All this is pleasant and convenient, and a great incitement to work in the field of history. It is equally true that a chronological approach works well with a variety of topics. Thus a paper on 'Poets of the 1914–18 War' might well deal with the host of names by grouping them around Brooke and Owen, representing the spirit (if one likes) of 1914 and 1917. This would be a fair start to the outline problem. Later one could face the question: does the quality and significance of the poetry of 1915–16 demand a section devoted to the transition?

(b) But chronology, unfortunately, is not the whole of history. The historians' problem also—and I take it as a model for anyone classifying material—is the ordering of events that occur simultaneously. To make their statements even approximately coherent, they must divide the activities of people into compartments labelled 'political', 'social', 'art', 'economics', etc. They must explain, as best they can, the interactions of these compartments. This analysis of life is artificial, like all analytical processes; and its justification is that the human mind can only communicate by imposing an artificial order on an incredibly complex mass of data. 'History', says Burckhardt, 'is the record of what one age finds notable in another.' Such is history; but the same act of judgement is necessary to select and order material in other fields.

Thus, the purely chronological outline I have mentioned in my first example is only apparently adequate. It is certainly a promising start. I doubt if a significantly better one could be devised. But it still leaves one with the problem of subdividing within the chronological framework. There the writer must search for an acceptable internal form.

In the speciment paper on Nazi Propaganda, reproduced below, the writer drew up a scheme combining chronology and analysis:

1. General definition of propaganda.
   Its relationship to the twentieth century.

2. Division of the role of Nazi Propaganda into three stages:

   (i) its role when they were a minority party;
   (ii) its role when they controlled the organs of government;
   (iii) war propaganda.

   The decision was then taken to exclude the third category.

This illustrates the ever-present need, mentioned at the beginning of this chapter, to exclude material, hitherto seen as promising and relevant.

3. Chronological treatment.

   (i) propaganda before 1933;
   (ii) propaganda after 1933.

   Within this framework the propaganda methods are to be examined separately for each section.

4. Questions raised by Nazi Propaganda.

In this example the starting-point is chronology but within that framework a further analysis has been found necessary.

(c) The title itself often affords some clue to the necessary internal form. Indeed, some writers will be well content with simply defining their paper's title. Take, for example, a title containing the term 'Primitive Art'. The term has to be defined before it can be applied; and the writer might well settle in the end for the title 'Some characteristics of Primitive Art'. The subject might be analysed thus:

1. Primitive art exists from earliest times.
   (*But* it is found among savage tribes today.)
2. It is crude, rough, unsophisticated.
   (*But* some primitive art is highly sophisticated.)
3. It is intimately connected with religious rites.
   (*But* how is this distinguished from later religious art?)
4. It is functionally connected with religion, having no base in self-expression.
   (*But* does the controlling purpose of primitive art negate the idea of self-expression?)
5. It represents nowadays a sophisticated and deliberate return to older methods of expression.
   (*But* is not this pseudo-Primitivism?)

Here the writer has laid out the ideas in accordance with a movement of sorts. The analysis moves from the obvious to the less obvious, early to modern. By the nature of the subject, not only the arguments but also the counter-arguments have to be considered. There is here a rough analytical framework that can serve either as a complete paper in itself, or as a starting point to a larger project. It is naturally possible to focus at length on any one point — say 4 — that seems the crux of the matter; reducing the other points to lesser issues that can be disposed of in the Introduction.

Generally, any difficulty inherent in the title should be faced *at once*. And in the above example the objections to each element in the analysis have been dealt with as they occur.

(d) One final example will serve to underline the need to analyse an issue into parts, and thus pave the way for a later synthesis. The student had taken the topic: 'The Flow of Traffic in Large Towns'. Clearly the title indicated a complex of unruly problems. The first step was to impose the simplest ordering of data, that is, 'Problems' and 'Solutions'. The next was to subdivide the problems, followed by the solutions. An outline of the paper looked like this:

I. *Introduction.* General statement of the problem.

II. *Aspects of the problem.*
    (a) Simultaneous use of local and through traffic.
    (b) Speed limits and traffic lights which slow down the flow.
    (c) Intersections.
    (d) Parked cars.
    (e) Loading and servicing of shopping areas.
    (f) Pedestrians, especially at crossings.

III. *Attempted Solutions.*

    (a) The Slough Experiment.
    (b) Various other solutions tried in Britain and abroad, as:
        (1) Urban motorways over, under or round the town to take traffic.
        (2) Roads from suburbs with tidal flow (three lanes in, one lane out, in the morning: and the converse in the evening).
        (3) Clover under- or over-passes for intersections or, where too expensive, computer-controlled traffic signals.
        (4) Multi-storey or underground off-street parking.

IV. *Conclusion.* General trends and prospects in the planners' fight to keep traffic moving.

The material here was refractory but a logical movement had again been observed. In the Problems, it was from roads and vehicles to people's use of them. In the Solutions, the breakdown was first broadly historical to take in the Slough Experiment, and then corresponded as far as possible to the analysis of the problems.

These examples cannot be reduced to a series of precepts. Every topic is a unique problem; it demands to be appraised in its own terms. What the student has to do is to develop the capacity to feel for the natural form inherent in every topic.

The student who is really anxious to develop this faculty, and there is none more important for really excellent work, will find it useful to study examples where it is displayed by others. Leading articles in the best journals and newspapers offer useful case material. One can also get into the habit of analysing the way material has been shaped for TV programmes. *Walden* on ITV is a useful example of a format which frequently moves from general exposition of a problem, in an introductory section, to the advancement of argument and counter-argument in a discussion or interview. A keen observation of the various methods used by experienced practitioners, to impose order and form on refractory material, will enable the student to develop his or her own skills.

The examples I have suggested here as case material are generally of limited length. More ambitious examples to follow can be found in the best reports of Select Committees, where a great bulk of material, collected over a fairly long period, and representing, of necessity, very opposing points of view, has to be rendered into clear, readable form, leading to clear recommendations.

A model of its kind, and worthy of study purely for its form, is the

*Warnock Report on Human Fertilisation and Embryology.** Here the writer, Dame Mary Warnock, was faced with a mass of difficult material involving technical definitions but also complex moral and legal issues. An exceedingly clear form was imposed on the Report.

Chapter 1 set out the background to the inquiry and its terms of reference, defined words used in the terms of reference, and divided the task into two parts. These were to consider (a) processes designed to benefit the individual and (b) the pursuit of knowledge designed to benefit society at large.

Thus a clear two-fold division was imposed at the start and this was followed, with chapters 2-8 concerned mainly with the first of these tasks and chapters 9-12 with the second.

Chapter 2 considered the state of infertility, whether it was a condition meriting treatment, and the scope of services for its alleviation. It drew the clear conclusion that it should be treated.

Chapter 3–8 considered, one by one, the possible techniques for doing this, the medical and legal questions involved with them, and the ethical arguments against. In the case of each technique clear definitions were given and a clear conclusion was drawn.

Chapter 9–12 shifted to the question of benefits to society at large, and considered the wider use of these techniques, both now and in the future. The scientific and moral implications raised by the use of human embryos for research were also addressed.

Chapter 13 gave clear recommendations for future policy.

Throughout the Report concentrated on principles rather than details, and made a clear distinction between areas where legislation would be needed, and those where only guidance or a general change of attitudes would be necessary. On the most difficult question of all, the moral dimension, the consistent approach throughout was that strongly, but not universally, held moral views are not binding on the formulation of public policy, since an individual holding them can refuse to participate in the particular practice under consideration.

A list of recommendations followed, with paragraph references to the relevant sections of the main text, thus binding the report together into a clear and consistent whole.

I have given a full analysis of this particular report because the material presents difficulties greater than any students can be expected to find in their own work. In particular the writer has to deal with a number of very technical issues, yet render them comprehensible to a lay readership. She has also to address herself to moral issues and give full weight to very

*Department of Health and Social Security, *Report of the Committee of Inquiry into Human Fertilisation and Embryology* (Chairman Dame Mary Warnock, DBE), presented to Parliament July 1984 (London: HMSO, 1984).

strongly held views which oppose the recommendations she finally advances. The consistency, clarity and logic of the argument throughout make it a model for students, and the fact that it is intended for a lay readership makes it useful as a model, even for those whose own studies may lie in a very different field.

Students may also, of course, find that there are government reports or similar official documents related to their own fields, in which they will find useful models for their own writing. It is the general principle that is important: to be alert to examples of good structure and to spend a few minutes analysing what it is that has made them good.

Writing the Rough Draft

With the outline prepared, the student should assemble the notes in readiness for the rough draft. They should be sorted out into the order corresponding to the outline's demands and the unwanted cards set aside. This decision should definitely precede the actual business of writing. There should be, at this stage, a clear-cut task of writing up a series of notes, in a predetermined order, into consecutive prose. It is worthwhile repeating here that the cards can easily be arranged into this order so that the writing becomes relatively simple.

Little need be said about this writing stage. As mentioned in the Introduction, I have no intention of telling my readers about basic composition. One point should, however, be made and that is the need to avoid giving offence by the use of 'he' and the variety of forms connected with it, when the reference could as well apply to a woman as a man. Since English is deficient in not possessing any form of neutral pronoun, other than 'one' which can become clumsy if repeated too often, considerable ingenuity needs to be exercised to overcome the problem. Students will find detailed guidance on the matter in the Appendix, pages 107–14.

Two practical suggestions on the writing stage ought to be considered. The student will be well advised to use wide-lined paper, or to write on alternate lines, to leave plenty of space for alterations or additions. Secondly, only one paragraph might be written on each sheet of paper, leaving space at the end for finishing incomplete paragraphs, or inserting additional material, afterthoughts, clarifying sentences, and so on. Certain long quotations may be referred to briefly and filled in later. Moreover, the whole paragraph may in the final version be assigned to a different part of the paper. Students who do not adopt this method should at least leave some spaces between each paragraph — and leave a considerable *margin*. One of the needless frustrations of revising a draft is to find no space available for afterthoughts.

In effect, by adopting the practices recommended above, the student is gaining some of the advantages offered by word processing. As technology is advancing so rapidly, many students will in fact have access to a word processor. If so they should certainly use it.

A word processor is the finest technical help to reshaping and reorganizing one's thoughts. One can type a rough draft rapidly, knowing that one can, with the utmost ease, make corrections, deletions and additions. One can also move whole paragraphs or sections around to improve the flow of the argument. There is no greater incentive to the improvement of formal structure and argument than the speed and ease with which this can be done.

I do not intend here to give any exposition of word processing techniques, since these will vary with the particular equipment and programs to which the student has access. I shall content myself with urging students to gain the benefit of this technology if they possibly can. One caution is worth advancing, and that is to be sure to 'save' the text on to tape or disc at frequent intervals, and to keep a back-up copy. There are few things as irritating as to have spent a couple of hours typing a text and then lose it, through a power cut before it is 'saved', or later, through loss of, or damage to, the disc.

Improving the Rough Draft

Turning the rough draft into the final draft is a business which needs a cold critical eye. I recommend that if possible the student should leave the rough draft for a while — Kipling left his for a year at a time — to grow 'cold'. A few days is better than nothing. It is vital to approach the rough draft as though it were someone else's. It might very well be read to a friend — Swift read his drafts to his servants, and Molière to his cook. The point of this is that it is psychologically very difficult to criticize one's own work. One's blind spots in composition tend to recur; and the tendency to approve one's own work is strong. But if the draft is 'cold' it is easier to approach it impartially; and an outside opinion is better still. In revising the rough draft, one ought to concentrate on two aspects: the verifying of footnotes, quotations and illustrations, and those aspects of the paper in which precision is essential; and the flow, and grammatical accuracy of the writing.

Getting ready one's footnotes, illustrations, etc., and checking their accuracy, needs no explanation. Nonetheless, the importance of this, labour is central. 'Accuracy', said Whitehead, 'is the morality of the scientist.' It is part of the morality of the researcher.

The quality of 'flow' stems naturally from a well-organized outline. But this in itself is not sufficient. The transition from paragraph to paragraph is an important technique. Usually, not invariably, the opening sentence of a paragraph — the 'topic sentence' — announces the theme of the paragraph to follow. Often it is possible to make the topic sentence link up with the last sentence of the preceding paragraph. Within the paragraph itself, a succession of guide words (such as 'however', 'consequently', 'on the other hand', 'moreover', 'thus', 'finally') help conduct the reader across the territory to be traversed. A well-written paper, in my view, is not so much one that is grammatically impeccable — that should be taken for granted — as one in which the chain of evidence and reasoning is easy to follow. No unreasonable demands should be made upon the reader. A common fault, for example, is for the researcher to become so immersed in the topic as to refer in the paper to personages, events, and terms that are obscure in the extreme. Unless one can assume a degree of expert knowledge in the reader, this is a provoking irritant. And it is courteous to remind even the enlightened reader. It is also a common fault of inexperienced writers to suppose that because they themselves know what they mean, their reader must automatically do so as well. Hence the value of reading the rough draft to a friend — and if that friend knows nothing of the topic, so much the better. The devastating interruption 'Who's he?' or 'What's that?' can remind the writer forcefully of the perennial duty to readers to make their lives as easy and pleasant as possible.

CHAPTER 5

The Final Version

Advice is given here in accordance with generally recognized practice, and especially with the recommendations of the Modern Humanities Research Association Style Book. It should be emphasized, however, that some institutions favour particular conventions. Publishers, for example, often have their own in-house style. Students must ensure that any particular regulations of their own institutions are followed. The advice given here is in default of such regulations being supplied.

One preliminary caution should be offered before any start is made on typing the final manuscript. Literary history abounds in cases of lost manuscripts. It can happen to anyone. The practice of taking a photocopy virtually eliminates the difficulties arising from such loss, and should always be followed. In any event, a copy has uses outside its insurance value; it enables the task of proof-reading to be shared, and permits a clean version of the text to be retained, free from marginalia.

Format

In its final form the research paper should be presented as a typescript. Conventionally the paper used is standard A4 (297 mm × 210 mm). The typing of the text should be double-spaced and as uniform as possible, in terms of line length and number of lines per page. A writer using a word processor may decide to have the smaller size fan-fold paper (278 mm × 217 mm), in order to enjoy the convenience of continuous printing, instead of having to insert individual sheets. The word processor will also, of course, give complete uniformity of line and page depth, and margin size, once the format has been decided. Whichever method is used, care must be taken to decide on a format which provides ample margins and ample top and bottom spaces. Allow 2 to 3 cm in each case, with the left-hand margin 4 cm wide, to allow for binding. The first page should have a margin of 5 cm at the top, and the title centred and typed in capitals. Pages should be numbered consecutively, either in the top right-hand corner, or in the centre at the top. It is a good plan to type one's own name before the number of each page, to guard against any of the pages being mislaid, or confused with those of another paper. The beginning of each new paragraph should be indented four spaces and the space between paragraphs should be the normal double-spacing, unless a decided break in subject matter is to be indicated.

Certain conventions of presentation should be observed throughout. Quotation marks are used to draw attention to a word or phrase which is under discussion, as: 'it is permissible to write "and others" after the name of the first author', where the words 'and others', are being singled out for consideration. If these words are used within a quotation, double quotation marks are used, otherwise single, as above. Where italics would be used for emphasis, if the full resources of the printer were available, a single underline should be employed. It should be noted, however, that too great a use of italics is out of keeping with a scholarly piece of work. A single underline should also be used for the titles of published works, and for foreign words used in the text, unless these are so much used as to have become anglicized. Usage for dates should be consistent. Practice varies, but the format 14 February, 1970 is gaining ground. The same consistency is required for numerals, where it is customary for those of fewer than three digits, and those beginning a sentence, to be spelled out.

Care must also be taken in the transcription of quotations. If the advice given above has been followed, the quotation will already be in the correct form on the note-card. It remains to insert it correctly into the text of the research paper. One must first distinguish between short quotations, fewer than sixty words of prose, and no more than two lines of verse, and longer quotations.

Short prose quotations may be run into the text without any introductory punctuation. They should be enclosed in single quotation marks. A quotation within a short quotation should be enclosed in double quotation marks. The question of the punctuation at the end of a quotation, in quotation marks, sometimes gives trouble. The rule is a simple one: if the punctuation is a necessary part of the original quotation, as in the case of a question mark or exclamation mark, it should be retained before the quotation marks. Otherwise the punctuation is that of the original sentence, in which the quotation is included, and comes after the quotation marks. This may, in fact, lead to double punctuation. Examples will make this clearer.

Examples

Who can deny the effectiveness of the description of Cleopatra as 'a lass unparalleled'?

(The quotation is not a question, therefore the question mark comes after the quotation marks, as part of the original sentence.)

We all remember Caesar's famous question 'Et tu, Brute?'.

(The quotation is a question, therefore the question mark comes before the quotation marks, and the original sentence is completed with its own full stop. If we turn this into a question, as below, we shall see the double punctuation more clearly:

> Which of us does not remember Caesar's famous question 'Et tu, Brute?'?

Short verse quotations are similarly run into the text. If the quotation extends over two lines, it is the practice to indicate the break, not by setting out, but by a slash followed by a capital letter, as in the following example:

> An example of this imagery is 'The hearts/That spaniel'd me at heels'.

Longer quotations must not be incorporated into a sentence in such a way as to break its continuity, since the reader cannot be expected to wait for the end of the sentence until after the quotation. They may, however, be introduced by a colon, indicating that they form an explanation, or extension, of the preceding sentence. They must begin on a new line. They are not enclosed in quotation marks. Some way must, therefore, be found of differentiating them from the main text. Practice on this varies, but the most frequently used method is to have a deeper indentation, often on both sides, and to use single spacing. Any quotation within the long quotation will be set off from it by single quotation marks, and, if there is a further quotation within that, by double quotation marks, following the rules given above for short quotations.

Long verse quotations present fewer problems, since they are already marked off by their form from a prose text. They also are typed without quotation marks, more fully indented, following their own verse or line format, and single spaced.

If it is desired to give a reference to the text, within the main body of the paper (line reference for verse or page reference), this is given in brackets, after the punctuation of the quotation, and with no punctuation of its own.

It is sometimes necessary to indicate, in the middle of a quotation, that material has been omitted. This is shown in prose quotations by three spaced full stops. In the case of verse quotations the three spaced full stops are typed at the end of the line before the omission.

The Preliminary Pages of Front Matter

The first page is the title page. This simply gives the details of title and author, and if required the name of the course and instructor. Next comes the outline. This is an abstract of the contents, prepared in complete sentence form. It should be an accurate summary of the main points established, while indicating the structure of the paper. Finally, it may be desirable to add a table of contents. Obviously, certain papers are fairly simple and written in continuous form. No table is here necessary. But if the paper is a more ambitious affair, containing chapters, illustrations, or appendixes, then a table of contents is in order.

Additional Material

The question of additional material (such as photographs, diagrams, graphs, statistical tables) must be briefly raised here. The presentation of such material, especially photographs, is a purely technical matter which must be left to the judgement of the writer. It is outside my brief to offer specific advice on this matter. I do, however, stress that the business of setting up illustrations should be taken very seriously. Illustrative material should be carefully chosen and prepared so as to give information. If, for example, a diagram relates specifically to a point explained in the text, it is sound policy to submit the text and diagram to a friend and ask: does the diagram, in fact, enlighten? Does it adequately complement the text? Is it, text aside, self-explanatory on its own visual terms? And this leads us to another consideration. Obviously the basic virtues of illustration are clarity and relevance. But the student should also consider the possibilities of sheer graphic appeal. Statistical information, for example, can be presented diagrammatically with great impact. Even a hoary old device such as depicting a single figure to represent a million of the population is better than nothing. It shows that the writer is making an effort to think graphically, to present information conceived visually, not tied to verbal forms. Such a faculty is not found universally, and many people are constricted by the heavily verbal emphasis of their formal education. They could well reflect on the opportunities a research paper affords to extend their range of expression. Even a simple graph is a case in point. It is not solely a mathematical concept; it is a visual device. The possibilities of a subject can and should be explored through visual means. It should also be noted that the technical possibilities of illustrating never were greater. Through the latest techniques of reproduction, colour, typography, and computer graphics, the student can intensify the projection of the theme.

A basic problem should be mentioned. Ought such material be presented alongside the text, often at the cost of considerable disarray? Or should it be relegated to the end of the paper, and presented in the form of an appendix or series of appendixes? Clearly the latter is more convenient for the writer; the former may be more convenient for the reader. The writer should ask the question: does the material throw any direct light upon the point considered in the text? Is it desirable for the reader to view with ease text and illustrations together? If so, then the writer should make an effort to accommodate the reader. But if the essential function of the illustrative material is to reinforce rather than to enlighten — this applies especially to statistical tables — then the writer should banish them to an appendix, and refuse to allow them to clutter up the text.

Documentation: Footnotes

The major problem in the final presentation of the text is the matter of documentation. The central issue is quite clear. The value of a research paper consists very largely in the sources used. Therefore, these sources must be acknowledged in two ways. The Bibliography listed at the end is a general acknowledgement; the footnotes spaced throughout the paper specifically and individually document facts and opinions referred to. Without this general and individual acknowledgement, the reader would be completely at sea. There would only be an unsubstantiated and undifferentiated mass.

What information should be documented via a footnote? The matter is quite considerably one of judgement. A fact like the date of the Battle of Waterloo requires no authority to support it. A fact like the casualty returns of the Prussians at Waterloo does. Facts in any way specialized or beyond the run of common knowledge ought to be documented. So should opinions. We ought to know the circumstances and the time when an opinion was formed. The time is particularly important as it often colours the views of the writer. (C. V. Wedgwood, for example, in the Introduction to the 1957 edition of her *The Thirty Years War* writes: 'I wrote this book in the thirties, against the background of depression at home and mounting tension abroad. The preoccupations of that unhappy time cast their shadows over its pages.') If the opinion being considered is a scholarly opinion, we must have the full details of the work cited. The authority should be cited, not left vague as 'one authority'. Clearly a direct quotation should always be footnoted. (Except the non-specialist allusion. One does not give chapter and verse for a quotation from *Hamlet*, unless one is writing on *Hamlet*.) A paraphrase of a quotation must also be footnoted. Finally, the sources of technical information such as tables, diagrams, charts, should also be acknowledged.

Conventions somewhat differ on the form the footnotes take. It is agreed that a single numeral, typed a single roller space above the line (and invariably at the *end* of the quotation or material to be documented, after punctuation, if any), should draw the reader's attention to the existence of the footnote. This numeral is then repeated at the foot of the page, or the end of the paper, and followed by a statement of the authority. But the numbering series can take various forms. It is permissible to number footnotes on a page-by-page basis: that is, given three footnotes on a page, one numbers 1, 2 and 3, then begins again with 1 on the next page. Or one can number them consecutively to the end of the section. Or one can number them consecutively throughout the whole paper, a method sometimes applied to entire books.

Practice varies also on the location of the footnotes. The term 'footnotes' is a sufficient indication of the normal placing of the notes. Still, there is a growing tendency for notes to be assembled either at the end of a chapter, or at the end of the entire work. Opinions differ on the usefulness of this tendency. It is certainly inconvenient to have to turn to another page for an authority. Yet a thicket of footnotes at the bottom of the page has little aesthetic appeal to the reader, especially when they afford only a mechanical liturgy of chapter and verse. Furthermore, it is troublesome to type a group of footnotes; one has to allow for the space needed, and it is painfully easy to forget the need for the space altogether. Typing the notes at the end is much easier. In my opinion the best solution is a compromise one. Some writers divide their notes into two categories. The first category contains the routine details of documentation — author, work, page number. The second embraces notes that are essentially explanatory — comment, additional quotation, illustrative material that cannot readily be absorbed into the main text. Category two should plainly be at the foot of the page; category one can safely be relegated to the end. This seems to me a sensible and civilized discrimination, and I recommend it to my readers. It does, however, assume a distinctive symbolism for each category of footnote. The writer adopting this division must be prepared to use an asterisk (or some other symbol) as opposed to numerals, to distinguish one category from the other.

If the writer prefers to adopt the method of typing footnotes at the foot of the page, certain points should be borne in mind. First, one may avoid the tiresome necessity of a string of footnotes referring to the same work, when part of the function of the paper is close study of that work. One may do this after the first full footnoted reference, by brief page references in parentheses in the main text, after the quotation marks. Thus if one is making a close study of Shakespeare's Sonnets, for example, after the first footnote giving full details of the edition used, one may give subsequent references by number and line, as: XVIII, 10-12. This saves tiresome repetition. A second point is that it is necessary to use a consistent format in the typing. It is recommended that the footnote should be set off from the text by allowing a triple space above and by single spacing the note itself. A double space should be left between footnotes. If for any reason the note cannot be completed on the page, it should be continued on the next page, separated from the text by a single continuous line, typed one space below the last line of the text. It is obvious that a careful calculation will be needed before the start of typing a page as to how much space will be needed for footnotes, to ensure that the last line of the last footnote is above the normal margin. When the calculation has been made, a tiny pencil mark in the margin, which can later be erased, will serve as a reminder where to stop typing the main text.

Whichever system of placing the footnotes is adopted, great care must be taken in maintaining the correct format for each footnote. This is where the material collected on the bibliography cards is first used. It is important to remember that there is a distinction between a first reference to a book or article, when the full version is used, and a subsequent reference when a streamlined version is sufficient.

First Reference Footnotes

The information is given as on the bibliography cards, but there are differences of format.

Reference to a book. The author's name is given first, in normal order, that is initials or first name(s), followed by last name, followed by a comma. This is followed by the title of the work, underlined, and followed by a comma, unless the facts of publication, which are enclosed in parentheses, immediately follow, in which case the comma follows the parentheses. If there is an editor or translator, if an edition other than the first is used, or if the book is one of a number of volumes, this information comes after the comma and before the publication details. Publication details are enclosed in parentheses. Usage varies on what is included. It is increasingly the practice to omit the publisher's name and to give only the place and date of publication. Students should take advice on the practice favoured by their own institutions, for example by consulting a recent unpublished thesis of that institution in the library. If the publisher's name is to be included, the form is as follows: place of publication, colon, name of publisher, comma, date of publication, exactly as on the bibliography card. The first example below illustrates this. If the publisher's name is not to be included, then the place of publication alone is given, followed by a comma and the date of publication, as in the other examples below. The parentheses are followed by a comma and then the exact location of the quotation, that is the volume number, if relevant, in Roman capitals, comma, page number(s), full stop.

Examples

Humphrey Carpenter, *OUDS: a Centenary History of the Oxford University Dramatic Society 1885–1985* (Oxford: Oxford University Press, 1985), p. 178.

The Backbench Diaries of Richard Crossman, edited by Janet Morgan (London, 1981), p. 316.

E. H. Gombrich, *The Story of Art*, 12th edition, enlarged and revised (London, 1972), p. 269.

C. J. Lowe and M. L. Dockrill, *The Mirage of Power*, 3 vols. (London, 1972), Vol. I, p. 18.

Reference to an article. The format used on the bibliography card should be followed exactly, except that the author's name is given in normal order and followed by a comma. Thus the second example given in Chapter 2 above, will be written:

Peter Arnott, 'Some Costume Conventions in Greek Tragedy', *Essays in Theatre*, Vol. 2, No. 1 (November 1983), pp. 3–18 (p. 15).

Second and Subsequent Reference Footnotes

All this refers to the first appearance of a footnote. Certain conventional short cuts are employed afterwards. Suppose that the first footnote is as the first example given above. The next footnote, if it refers to the same work, need not repeat the information. It is now no longer the accepted practice to use the abbreviation of the Latin forms (*ibid.* for *ibidem* 'in the same place', and *op. cit.* for *opere citato* 'in the work cited'). Instead, it is recommended practice to give the author's name and the page reference, if only one work by that author is being cited. Thus for the first example above, one would write Carpenter, p. 105. If one is referring to more than one work by the same author, it will be necessary to give a shortened form of the title. If, for example, one were using two books by Emrys Jones, say *Scenic Form in Shakespeare* and *The Origins of Shakespeare*, one might, after the first full reference footnote, use Jones, *Origins*, p. 50, and Jones, *Scenic Form*, p. 85, to distinguish them.

Where close study of a particular text is carried on throughout one or more paragraphs, it is possible to incorporate page references in brackets within the text, and thus avoid a string of repetitive footnotes. In the Specimen Paper, for example, the writer has incorporated bracketed references to *Mein Kampf* into her text.

Documentation: Bibliography

To the Bibliography belongs the place of honour at the rear of the research paper. It comes last, following the main text, the Appendixes (if any), and the Notes (if they have been assembled at the end, and not typed as footnotes). It is a formal statement of the credentials of the paper, and should be presented in the fullest and most exact form possible. Moreover, it should be honest. There are lies, damned lies, and bibliographies: it is easy to draw up an imposing list of titles known more by repute than otherwise to the writer. The criterion for inclusion, however, is clear. The Bibliography (in effect the final Bibliography) should include only those sources which the researcher has actually used for the paper. It is thus different from the initial Bibliography, which was purely a stage in the preparation of the paper, and listed all possible sources. The final Bibliography lists only those sources which yielded significant material to the researcher. This does not mean that only sources actually quoted in the paper may be cited. One might, for example, read a book as important background material, yet find no opportunity of actually working part of it into one's paper, even though it has significantly enlarged one's understanding of the topic. Or one might study an obviously relevant source book, yet draw a blank as far as usable material goes; a great deal of honest research may afford only negative conclusions. In either case it is perfectly proper to cite the works one has consulted. Again, one may use only a chapter, or a part, of a work. The great thing is that the Bibliography should cite only material genuinely relevant to the topic, and genuinely consulted by the researcher.

The Form of the Bibliography

Again, the details are taken from the bibliography cards. The student will now see why the information on these cards is not quite in the same format as that used for the footnotes. The bibliography card has the author's name with last name first; this makes for ease of sorting for the Bibliography which is always presented in alphabetical order.

All items should be listed alphabetically by the last name of the author or editor. A work which has both author and editor will be listed under author, unless it is the qualities of the editing which the paper has been considering. If no author's or editor's name is available, but the work is produced by a public body, it is listed under the first important word of their name. If not even this is available, it is listed under the first important word of the title. Several titles by the same author should also be listed alphabetically from the first important word in each title. This simple classification ought to be enough for a research paper; however, sometimes a mass of detail invites a further classification. One can conveniently distinguish between books and articles. Often a Bibliography is divided into 'General' works and materials specifically related to the topic. Historians especially like to distinguish between primary and secondary sources. And the nature of the topic frequently suggests its own breakdown into areas. For the great majority of student papers, however, a simple alphabetized list will be sufficient.

The details given are exactly the same as in the footnotes, but with differences of format. Thus the author's name, or the first author's name, if there is more than one, is given with the last name first, followed by a comma, followed by the first name(s) or initials, exactly as on the bibliography cards. The title is underlined, in the case of a book, or placed in single quotation marks, in the case of an article. Publishing details are given as on the bibliography card. On the question of punctuation and setting out of these details usage again varies. The important thing is to be consistent in whatever style one has chosen to adopt. Again, students are advised to check what is the preferred style of their own institutions. The two areas of difference are in the separation of the author's name from the title, and the way that the publishing details are set off from the rest. Some authorities use a comma to separate author's name from the title of the work and others use a full stop. In general, Americans recommend the full stop, but many English authorities prefer the comma. In the absence of a ruling from one's own institution, one may choose either form, but the important thing is that having chosen, one should stick to it. The same goes for publication details. Some prefer to retain the bracketed form as used in the footnotes, while others remove the brackets and separate the publishing details from the rest by using a full stop. Again, as for the footnotes, the publishing details may include or omit the name of the publisher. In setting out the complete bibliography, it is normal practice to indent the second and subsequent lines of each entry. Examples will make clear the different possible forms.

Example of one entry under different forms

Olivier, Laurence. *Confessions of an Actor.* London: Weidenfeld and
    Nicolson, 1982.
Olivier, Laurence, *Confessions of an Actor* (London: Weidenfeld and
    Nicolson, 1982).

In each case, publishing details could be shortened, by the omission of the publishers' name, to London, 1982.

These, then, are the possible variations in format. I give below a list of examples of different kinds of entries, using the first form.

Examples of different kinds of entries

(1. A book by a single author.)

Morris, Jan. *The Venetian Empire: A Sea Voyage.* London, 1980.

(2. A book by two authors.)

Middlemass, Keith, and John Barnes. *Baldwin: A biography.* London,
    1969.
(*Note*: The name of the second author is not inverted, since it does not affect the alphabetical placing.)

(3. A book by several authors.)

Parker, Geoffrey, and others. *The Thirty Years War.* London, 1984.

(4. An edition of an author's works.)

Marvell, Andrew. *The Poems and Letters of Andrew Marvell*, ed. H. M. Margoliouth, 2 vols. 2nd ed. Oxford, 1952.

(5. An anthology or edited collection.)

Keating, Peter, ed. *The Victorian Prophets: A Reader from Carlyle to Wells*. Glasgow, 1981.

(6. A translation.)

Virgil. *The Aeneid*, trans. W. F. Jackson Knight. Harmondsworth, 1956.

(7. An article in a journal.)

Brittan, Samuel. 'Hayek, the New Right, and the Crisis of Social Democracy', *Encounter*, Vol. 54, No. 1 (January 1980), pp. 31–46.

(8. An article in an edited collection.)

Vernon, M. D. 'Attention and Visual Perception', in *Readings in Psychology*, ed. John Cohen. London, 1964.

(9. An article in an Encyclopedia.)

'Numismatics', *Encyclopedia Britannica*, vol. XV, pp. 615–634. 1964.

(10. A newspaper article.)

Chester, Lewis. 'The Truth about Beveridge', *Sunday Times*, 9 June 1985, p. 18.

(11. A pamphlet or guide.)

Guide to the British Museum. London, 1965.

For further examples of footnotes and bibliographical entries, and the difference in form between them, the student is advised to study the Specimen paper (Chapter 6).

CHAPTER 6

Specimen Paper

This chapter consists of a paper written by an M.A. student and used with her permission. It illustrates most of the principles that have been outlined in this book, and provides illustrations of footnotes and Bibliography in practice. The length of this paper is naturally no guide to students, any more than the number of footnotes or Bibliographical entries. These matters will be determined by the nature and requirements of each paper.

NAZI PROPAGANDA

BY

Instructor.....................

Course........................

Date..........................

Abstract: Nazi Propaganda

Purpose. This paper examines the role of propaganda
in the Nazi Party and government, its aims and methods,
and some of the questions it raises.

Introduction. A general consideration of various
definitions of propaganda and of its role in the Nazi
success in Germany.

Section I. Nazi propaganda in the period of the Party's
rise to power.

Section II. Nazi propaganda in the period from 1933
to the outbreak of war, when they had control of all
the organs of the state.

Section III. Some questions and conclusions raised
by a consideration of Nazi propaganda.

NAZI PROPAGANDA

Introduction

Propaganda is so central to the Nazi system that
it is hardly possible to talk of that system without
the word cropping up in the first few sentences. When
we ask how did this movement get a grip on a great,
cultured European nation, it is all too easy to reply
at once 'Propaganda'. But is it really as simple as
that? It is the intention of this paper to examine
the aims and methods of Nazi Propaganda and then, in
the light of this examination, to consider certain
fundamental questions it raises.

First, it is necessary to consider what propaganda
is. Propaganda has existed from time immemorial in
an unsystematic sense embracing the various means by
which governments from ancient times have succeeded
in riveting the allegiance of the governed. The word
itself is of comparatively recent origin. The Oxford
English Dictionary gives its derivation from an
association of the Roman Catholic Church de propaganda
fide for propagating the faith. The first usage
quoted is in 1842 when it is said to be 'applied in
modern political language as a term of reproach to
secret associations for the spread of opinions and
principles which are viewed by most governments with
horror and aversion'. Thus already it had acquired
the pejorative sense which was to cling to it. The
O.E.D., however, is studiously neutral in its own
definition: 'Any association, systematic scheme, or
concerted movement for the propagation of a particular
doctrine or practice.'

But, if propaganda has a long history, it is
generally acknowledged that propaganda as we think
of it is the creation of the twentieth century. It
required certain conditions for its successful
application which only the twentieth century has
produced: the industrial and urban society which draws

large numbers of people together, at the same time
as it shatters old stable relationships and fragments
society; mass literacy; and the technical means of
mass communication and suggestion. It can be no
coincidence that totalitarian regimes have built on
these conditions propaganda machines of immense success.
The Nazi system was the first to use all modern means
of communication to the full, to elevate propaganda
into a science in itself, based on the sciences of
sociology and psychology, and to convert the entire
machinery of social and cultural life into one vast
propaganda machine. 'Propaganda is an inalienable
and vital function of the modern state', Goebbels
declared.[1] As such it achieved a considerable success,
at least as far as the Hitler cult was concerned. It
has been many times remarked that the regime was over-
thrown in the end by external war, not by internal
strains or revolution.[2] Indeed, a study showed that
from June 1944 to April 1945 more than 60% of German
soldiers retained their faith in Hitler. Moreover,
despite the fact that in the last four months of the
war communications were cut off, and police and party
pressures were sporadic, resistance to the allies
continued, and there was none of the internal collapse
of 1918, showing that the people had been 'propagandised
in depth'.[3]

    It would perhaps be useful here to examine another
definition of propaganda which takes these twentieth-
century characteristics into account. Jacques Ellul,
in his perceptive study Propaganda, gives this definition,
which he qualifies as only partial: 'propaganda is
a set of methods employed by an organized group that
wants to bring about the active or passive participation
in its actions of a mass of individuals, psychologically
unified through psychological manipulations and incorporated in an organization'.[4] This is a much better
working definition when one is examining Nazi propaganda.
It has been enlarged to include not only opinions but
actions, and it conveys the ideas of the psychological,
or irrational, means, and of the psychologically unified
mass which are so central to its success. Goebbels
wrote of the Ministry for Popular Enlightenment and

Propaganda, 'I see the first task of this new ministry
as establishing a coordination between the Government
and the whole people.'[5] The effects of this, and the
methods used, will be examined more fully in Section
II below.

It is possible to distinguish three stages in
Nazi propaganda: first its use in their rise to power
from tiny beginnings to that of an important minority
party; second its use when they had control of government,
and therefore the organs to impose their will fully;
and third when they were at war. Since the problems
of war propaganda are much the same for all countries
and the Nazis were less innovative in that respect,
I propose to confine myself in this paper to the first
two. In the first period the seeds of most of the
later Nazi propaganda methods were sown, but they
required control of all the organs of the state to
come to full fruition.

Section I: The Propaganda of the Minority Party

It is impossible in reading Mein Kampf[6] not to
be amazed at the conscious, sure, developed grasp of
mass manipulation which it reveals, all the more
amazing when one considers that Volume I was published
in 1925 and Volume II in 1926. It is on this that
much of Hitler's reputation for 'political genius'
rests. A quite disproportionate amount of the book
is given to an exposition of propaganda methods; he
reverts to it over and over again, showing the depth
of his interest, and many of what might be called his
more political ideas seem shaped to propaganda ends,
a point to which I shall return at the end of this
paper. Moreover, it is these sections of the book
which have most vitality. As Alan Bullock puts it,
they 'stand out in brilliant contrast with the turgid
attempts to explain his entirely unoriginal ideas'.[7]
Hitler gives a detailed exposition of the methods to
be followed, but at its heart lie two interconnected
principles: the appeal was to be to the broad masses,
and, for this reason, it was to be to the emotions,

to the irrational element, and not to the intellect.
Because the appeal was to be to the masses it was to
be simplified and expressed in very black and white
terms, with constant repetition. 'As soon as our own
propaganda admits so much as a glimmer of right on
the other side, the foundation for doubt in our own
right has been laid' (p. 183); 'the art of all truly
great national leaders . . . consists . . . in not
dividing the attention of a people, but in concentrating
it upon a single foe. . . . It belongs to the genius
of a great leader to make even adversaries far removed
from one another seem to belong to the same category.
. . . Once the wavering mass sees itself in a struggle
against too many enemies objectivity will put in an
appearance. . . .' (p. 118) 'Faith is harder to shake
than knowledge, love succumbs less to change than respect,
hate is more enduring than aversion. . . . Anyone
who wants to win the broad masses must know the key
that opens the door to their heart. Its name is not
objectivity (read weakness) but will and power.'
(pp. 337-338)

In achieving this appeal to the emotions rather
than the intellect Hitler relied upon 'the magic power
of the spoken word . . . the firebrand of the word . . .
a storm of hot passion' (p. 107), of which he himself
was a consummate master, and which he felt was self-
correcting in a way that the written word addressed
to impersonal and unknown readers would never be. The
speaker 'will always let himself be borne by the great
masses in such a way that instinctively the very words
come to his lips that he needs to speak to the hearts
of the audience. And if he errs, even in the slightest,
he has a living correction before him.' (p. 470) How
accomplished he was in this respect has been asserted by
Otto Strasser: 'Hitler responds to the vibrations of the
human heart with the delicacy of a seismograph. . . .
Adolf Hitler enters a hall. He sniffs the air. For a
minute he gropes, feels his way, senses the atmosphere.
Suddenly he bursts forth. His words go like an arrow to
their target, he touches each private wound on the raw,
liberating the mass unconscious, expressing its inner-
most aspirations, telling it what it most wants to
hear.'[8] It is interesting in this regard to notice

that, while the radio was used by Hitler to great effect, he made few live broadcasts but relied instead on recordings of speeches actually delivered, where he could secure the response of a live audience.[9]

Hitler deliberately directed his appeal to the emotions, including that of physical terror. It has been many times pointed out that Nazism bears all the marks of a perverted religion, a religion of hate, not love, with the 'rhetoric of hell', and with all the symbolism of religion,[10] and Hitler admits to having borrowed from the Roman Catholic Church with its mysterious twilight, burning lamps, incense, etc. He was to use these devices in his mass meetings, to be held at night when the power to resist a stronger will is lowered. Hitler saw in his mass meetings the key to winning over the fragmented individual by incorporating him or her into an immensely strong whole. His metaphors for this are extraordinarily vivid:

> The gigantic demonstrations, these parades of hundreds of thousands of men, which burned into the small wretched individual the proud conviction that, paltry worm as he was, he was nevertheless a part of the great dragon, beneath whose burning breath the hated bourgeois world would some day go up in fire and flame and the proletarian dictatorship would celebrate its ultimate final victory. (p. 473)

> When from his little workshop or big factory, in which he feels very small, he steps for the first time into a mass meeting and has thousands of people of the same opinions around him. . . . The will, the longing and also the power of thousands are accumulated in every individual. The man who enters such a meeting doubting and wavering leaves it inwardly reinforced. He has become a link with the community. (p. 479)

To reinforce this sense of community Hitler used participation to the full. The Labour Service units,

and others at the rallies, were trained in choric
speaking, and the many collections of documents on
Nazism offer repeated evidence of the infectious
enthusiasm conveyed by the refrain of Sieg Heil.[11]

Hitler also had great faith in the emotional power
of symbolism. He described the effect on him of seeing
in a pre-war Marxist meeting 'the suggestive magic
of spectacle', 'a sea of red flags, red scarves and
red flowers' (p. 492). He himself adopted the swastika
as a symbol, and designed the red, black and white
flag incorporating it, and the standards which were
to be potent symbols of Nazism.

Thus, by 1925, Hitler, who had been appointed
in 1920 to direct the propaganda of the infant party,
had already shown a firm grasp of the essentials he
was to use. In that year he first met Dr. Joseph Goebbels
the other great master of propaganda, and almost his
equal in oratory. In the following year Goebbels was
made Gauleiter of Berlin and began to develop the methods
of propaganda which were to help the Nazis to electoral
successes in the Depression period. In 1930 he was
appointed to head the central Propaganda Department
in the Party H.Q. at Munich.

All the elements were there, though for the present
they could be used in only a limited way. The party
had a network of local organizations and its own press.
Its national newspaper, the Völkischer Beobachter,
became a daily paper in 1923. In 1929 its circulation
was only 18,400. With the Depression there was a big
growth to 128,000 in 1931, but its circulation became
large only with the Nazi assumption of power. In 1932
the Nazi press consisted of 59 daily journals, but
their combined circulation was only about three-quarters
of a million.[12] Many of them were 'violent in
language . . . crude almost beyond belief. The worst
of them scarcely resembled a weekly newspaper but rather
a badly printed brochure of ten to twenty pages filled
with the wildest and meanest diatribes.'[13] But, bad
as they were, they served as party organs and
disseminators of party propaganda. At election times

their print order was increased and many were distributed free.[14]

The uniforms of the S.A. men, the swastika symbol,
the flags, the military parades and constant meetings
utilized the military spirit and created a feeling of
omnipresence, and of greater numbers than the movement
could actually claim.[15]   Goebbels early realized the
importance of what he called 'the conquest of the streets'.
In the new mass age the street was 'the criterion of
modern politics. He who can conquer the streets can
also conquer the masses.'[16]   Thus meetings were announced
and held in a deliberately provocative manner to
encourage street brawls and violence. By this means
several objects were achieved: physical terror was used,
as Hitler had advocated; the Nazis presented themselves
as numerous, vigorous and activist; and politics became
irrationalized.[17]

In organizing their meetings the Nazis showed
particular skill in appealing to sectional and economic
interests. They created smaller organizations for
occupational groups, the members of which were able
to propagandize their colleagues. They also exploited
local issues and interests. In W. S. Allen's 'Thalburg'
(the name he gave, for reasons of confidentiality, to
the small town in Germany of which he had done a thorough
study), with its high proportion of government employees,
they announced a meeting on 'Civil Service and National
Socialism', and held other meetings devoted to the
interests of artisans, businessmen, civil servants,
pensioners and workmen.[18]

Though they were not yet able to make that thorough
assault on youth and education that governmental power
made possible, the Nazis had made a beginning there
also. The Hitler Youth was founded in 1926, though
by 1932 its total enrolment was only 107,956, as compared
with about ten million in other youth organizations.[19]
But the small numbers somewhat belie the potentiality
for influence of the movement. A youth described his
reasons for joining in 1930 thus: 'I wanted to be in
a boys' club where I could strive towards a national-

istic ideal. The Hitler youth had camping, hikes, and
group meetings. . . .   There were no social or class
distinctions. . . .   We weren't fully conscious of what
we were doing but we enjoyed ourselves and also felt
important.'[20]   The potential menace of the movement
was felt by those concerned with the growth of Nazism
in the Protestant Youth movement: 'certainly 70% of
our young people, often lacking knowledge of the facts
are in ardent sympathy'. 'Fifth formers are not really
much concerned with the study of Hitler's thoughts;
it is simply something irrational, something infectious
that makes the blood pulse through one's veins and
conveys an impression that something great is under
way. . . .' A complaint of 1930 in Oldenburg of Hitler
Youth intimidating other pupils in the school goes on
to reveal that many of the teachers are National
Socialists or sympathizers and cannot be relied on to
stop it. 'The relationship of trust necessary between
teachers and parents and their children has completely
gone.'[21]

In all this building up of specialist groups,
business, youth, etc., the Nazis foreshadowed their
later takeover of all clubs and associations in Germany.

As with the Press so with the other mass media,
the Nazis were able to make only limited use of them.
Goebbels had an imaginative grasp of the potentiality
of the mass media. The originality of his concepts
can be shown by two examples. The first is his very
'modern' campaign of a sequence of three posters for
his paper Der Angriff (The Attack):

The Attack?

The attack takes place on July 4th.

And finally, when curiosity had been fully aroused,
the announcement that The Attack was a new German Monday
newspaper.

The second example is his ingenious use of recording.

In the 1932 campaign, he had challenged Chancellor
Brüning to appear for a public debate on the same platform with him. On his refusal, Goebbels had one of
his radio speeches recorded and played it, with frequent
interruptions for himself to challenge or question his
invisible and 'speechless' opponent. 'The public was
in a rage of enthusiasm.'[22] This gives some idea of
what Goebbels might have done with the government
controlled radio, if at his disposal in those early
years. Goebbels also realized the power of film for
propaganda, but in the early years the party's tiny
film unit could make only amateurish films for private
showing at party meetings, and shared with other parties
the advantage of having its mass rallies featured
occasionally in the news reels.

With Hitler's highly developed sense of the
importance of the spectacle, pageantry, ritual and the
mass meeting, it is not surprising that the Nuremberg
rallies were an early development. The first party
rally was held in Munich in 1923, and from the beginning
much of the ceremonial of the ritual consecration of
the flags and the march past was established. From
then on, including a second one in the same year, rallies
were held mainly in Nuremberg, chosen as symbolic of
the Nazi fusion of past and present. Nuremberg was
a medieval city in pure German style, associated with
Dürer and other German artists, and made famous by its
rediscovery during the German Romantic Movement. It
was heavily publicized by the Nazis in a big propaganda
campaign in newspapers and magazines. Further rallies
were held in 1926, 1927 and 1929. Membership of the
Party rose from 17,000 in 1926 to 40,000 in 1927, and
the rally of 1927 was the first big demonstration of
its strength. Hitler took the salute at a torchlight
procession of about 30,000 brownshirts, and it is
estimated that 160,000 people attended the rally.[23]

In the 1932 election campaign, with the acquisition
of more funds, the Nazi propaganda machine showed what
it could do. Even the smallest villages were canvassed.
Films of Hitler and Goebbels were made and shown.
50,000 gramophone records were distributed by Goebbels'

Department and use was made of recorded speeches played
by loudspeaker vans, as a substitute for the radio which
they did not control. But the greatest effort, as might
be expected from Hitler's belief in the power of the
spoken word, responsive to the living audience, was
put into mass meetings, in which the Nazi orators stirred
the people to frenzied enthusiasm. Goebbels made nine-
teen speeches in Berlin, besides those he made in other
towns, while Hitler addressed audiences of up to 100,000,
taking advantage of the microphones which had become
standard equipment at Nazi meetings from 1930.[24]

Despite all this effort Hitler's vote was only
11 million to Hindenburg's 18 million, and in Berlin
he came third. Hindenburg did not secure the necessary
absolute majority, however, and another election had
to be held. Here Goebbels showed his ingenuity in
propaganda when he used the device of having Hitler
travel across Germany by plane with the inspiring slogan
'Hitler over Germany'. This had several effects:
Hitler spoke directly to about a million people; he
took advantage of the public interest in the novelty
of aviation, creating interest and enthusiasm by speaking
in three of four widely separated cities on the same
day; and he utilized the almost mythic effect of arrival
by air.[25] Goebbels' superb press organization took
full advantage of this, especially the fortuitous fact
that Hitler's plane took off for Düsseldorf in a violent
storm when all other air traffic was grounded. This
episode was later used to great effect in a propaganda
school text.[26]

By these ingenious means, and the sheer sustained
effort of their campaign, they pushed Hitler's vote
up another 2 million, though Hindenburg with 19 million
easily obtained his absolute majority. In the other
elections of 1932 the Nazi Party kept up its pressure.
In July, in his third flight over Germany, Hitler visited
fifty towns. Bullock gives the figures for his share
of the vote as rising from 30% in March to 37.3% in
July, and falling to 33.1% in November, with a drop
of 40%, from the July figure, in a later local election
in Thuringia.[27] This is the strongest argument for

a belief that in a fair field with no favour, Nazi
propaganda was not enough, that with the Depression
lessening and the particular constellation of events
which had led to their big increase in support dying
away, they had 'peaked' already.

Section II: The Propaganda of Government

The appointment of Hitler as Chancellor in 1933
was to give the Nazis the full power of the State to
create a new system of total propaganda. 'Nazi ideology
tried to claim the whole man - in his political, economic,
social and even private life. Propaganda therefore
had the function of creating a "new" man and a "new"
society.'[28] Now at last Hitler had the opportunity
to abolish the dreaded 'objectivity', to ensure that
all voices were silenced, save one, and that a cultural
and intellectual wall was built round Germany within
which only an approved set of ideas flourished.

Goebbels was made head of the Ministry of Popular
Enlightenment and Propaganda, whose work was subdivided
into many departments, but unified by its total scope
and one-man control. The number of divisions varied,
growing to fourteen by 1942, but an idea of their all-
embracing quality can be gathered from this list for
1936:

Division I: Legislation and legal problems; Budget,
Finances, and Accounting; Personnel Administration;
Ministerial Library; National Chamber of Culture;
Council of Commercial Advertising; Fairs and
Expositions.

Division II: Coordination of Popular Enlightenment
and Propaganda; Regional Agencies of the Ministry;
German Academy of Politics; Official Ceremonies
and Demonstrations; National Emblems; Racial
Questions; Treaty of Versailles; National Literature
and Publishing; Opposing Ideologies; Youth
Organization; Business and Social Politics; Public
Health and Athletics; Eastern and Border Questions;

National Travel Committee.

Division III: Radio; National Broadcasting Company.

Division IV: National and Foreign Press; Journalism;
Press Archives; News Service; National Association
of the German Press.

Division V: Cinema; Moving Picture Industry; Cinema
Censorship; Youth Literature Censorship.

Division VI: Theatre, Music, and Art; Theatre
Management; Stage Direction; Design; Folk Art.

Division VII: Protection against Counter-Propaganda
at Home and Abroad.[29]

I have reproduced this somewhat lengthy list because it
illustrates clearly the determination of the propagandists
to leave no channel unfilled with their propaganda,
nor free for anyone else's ideas. The list is nothing
if not exhaustive.

Swiftly the State secured total control of the mass
media. The Nazis secured a totally subservient press
by a number of steps. First, in 1933, they closed down
Socialist and Communist papers, confiscating their plant,
and took over the Reich Association of the German Press.
All journalists and editors were required to belong
to it and screened for 'racial and political reliability'.
The Editors Law of 1933 made the editors quasi-state
officials, responsible for the content of their papers
while the publishers became mere business managers.
Clear directives were issued to the Press and were secret
and absolutely binding. In 1933 and 1934 the Nazi papers
were brought under the Nazi publishing house Eher Verlag,
under the Reich Leader for the Party Press, Max Amann.
But this was not enough: the papers with a heavy national
circulation were still privately owned. At the end
of 1934 the party-owned papers had barely 25% of total
circulation.[31] The Nazi attitude is revealed in this
memorandum:

The National Socialist <u>Weltanschauung</u> demands
total acceptance and does not tolerate the
propagation of other basic ideas. On this
basis a state whose foundation is the National
Socialist movement recognizes only a National
Socialist Press.[32]

Thus in 1935 the Amann Decrees, of very comprehensive
scope struck at all trade and religious papers; all
papers in areas where there was too much competition;
and all produced by corporations, or persons with major
interests outside the publishing field, in effect all
the big newspaper chains. In the next eighteen months
500 or 600 papers disappeared or merged. By 1939 the
party-owned and controlled press held about two-thirds
of the total circulation, the 2,000 privately owned
papers the other one-third.[33] Even within this framework the Nazis secured tighter control through the
Reich Press Chief, Otto Dietrich. Daily, or twice daily,
the editors were called to a Press Conference where
they were handed '10 or 12 closely typed pages, containing many prohibitions and few permissions. It
prescribed the treatment of the specified themes with
regard to space, tone, headlines, and placement down
to the last detail.' Even the words to be used were
prescribed: 'From 1933 onwards editors became more
and more rubber stamps for officially stated views.'[34]

Amann said the editors complained they received a one-
inch file of news and a three-inch file of directives.[35]
Under the circumstances circulation dropped and Goebbels
was continually calling for the more imaginative treatment and more originality needed to raise it, which
his own self-defeating policy prevented. He complained
in 1936 of those who stopped buying a paper: 'These
people are not now reached by any newspaper and have
therefore been quite inadequately influenced by the
state and the party.'[36] But despite a big advertising
campaign he could not win them back until the war
created a demand for news and hence rising circulation.
This illustrates a recurring difficulty of the Ministry
of Propaganda: the State might control the media but
how far could it force people to absorb unpalatable

material?   This is a point to which I shall return in the final section of the paper.

It was otherwise, however, with radio.   Here the Nazi control was effective.   It was already well set up to take over since, in 1926, the Ministry of Posts held 51% of the stock of the National Broadcasting Company and there was a supervisory committee of three to scrutinize programme content.   By the end of 1933 all provincial radio companies were dissolved and the national government had taken over all radio facilities.[37] Moreover, it put pressure on manufacturers to produce cheap sets.   By the beginning of the war a set was produced for under £3 and it was estimated that 70% of households had one.   The cheap set in Germany was deliberately designed to pick up only German stations.[38] Lest even the remaining segment of the population should escape, or those with sets exercise their privilege of failing to listen, an elaborate system of wireless wardens was set up.

> It is the duty of these men to organise reception; they must see that every school and public square, coffee house, theatre and factory is fitted with receivers and amplifiers which make community reception possible.   At times of important broad-casts, all work is stopped.   Shops are closed. The flow of traffic, which might cause inter-ference, ceases.   It has been estimated that about 75% of the population hears the official transmission upon such occasions.[39]

This captive audience was offered programming carefully planned to foster National Socialist ideas. From overt propaganda in the sense of direct speeches, government proclamations, talks on history from the Nazi point of view or on racial doctrines, through lectures on military subjects and military music, to folklore, German music and glowing descriptions of the German countryside, nothing was neglected that would build up the right world view.   Programming was even carefully synchronized with workers' lunch and break times in factories, and the wireless wardens were to

forward listener response. Care was taken to use the
medium for the maximum effect. In 1933 Hitler spoke
to the nation for 45 minutes from the Siemens electric
plant, standing on a dynamo, surrounded by workers,
heralded by shrieking sirens and the roar of machinery.[40]
There was an even more impressive use of sound effects
in a broadcast from Nuremberg in September 1938.

> On a foundation of Wagnerian music there was
> heard a daunting rumbling, slow and emphatic of
> drums, and heavy footfalls pounding the earth,
> together with an indescribable rattle and swish
> and pant of armed masses on the march. This
> noise, now growing, now receding, must have
> clutched at the hearts of the millions of listeners,
> filling them with apprehension of disaster - a
> feeling of fascination and fear, deliberately
> produced by the men who staged the spectacle. . . .
> This was 100 per cent Hitlerist propaganda, an
> attempt to intimidate, to subject the millions
> of listeners in the world to psychical violation.[41]

This is a far cry indeed from the fireside chats of
Roosevelt, and the low-key discourses of Baldwin, pipe
in hand.

It is worth spending a little time on radio
because this was the method par excellence by which
the Nazi regime reached the masses.[42] It was the nearest
Hitler could get to making the whole nation the audience
for his 'magic power of the spoken word',[43] and by the
method I have outlined above, of broadcasting speeches
delivered before live audiences, he could still secure
the 'living correction' of the live audience. The
audiences for Hitler's big speeches have been variously
estimated at from 56 to 80 million, including, of
course, some from outside Germany.

The Nazis also controlled the film industry. In
1933 the Aryan clause banned Jews from any part of the
industry and some of the best artists began to emigrate.
In 1934 only members of the Reichsfilmkammer were allowed
to produce films and there was an all-inclusive

censorship decree. At the same time foreign films
with Jewish artists were banned, as were those with
unacceptable content. Censorship was interpreted in
the narrowest possible way, since not only what was
unacceptable in terms of political and ideological
content was disallowed, but also anything which went
against the narrow and somewhat old-fashioned morality
of the Nazi view. In the circumstances it is not
surprising that the German film industry declined and
its non-propaganda products became empty of content
and essentially escapist. Only a small number of
strictly propaganda films was made, since the German
people had to be induced to pay to go to the cinema and
showed a lack of desire to see propaganda films.
'Goebbels believed that propaganda was most effective
when it was insidious, when its message was concealed
within the framework of popular entertainment.'[44]
But this proved difficult to achieve. It proved more
successful to rely on short films and newsreels for
propaganda, and to use the pulling power of the feature
film. To ensure a captive audience after 1941 it was
common practice to lock the doors of the cinema during
the showing of newsreels.[45] Of about 1,363 feature
films under the Third Reich, 208 were banned after the
war by various Allied Governments for containing
propaganda, many of them on rather slight grounds.[46]
The most successful propagandist film maker, who
combined entertainment with a strong propagandist line,
urging sacrifice for country, or denigrating democracy,
was Karl Ritter. He declared, 'I want to show German
youth that senseless, sacrificial death has its moral
value', and it is estimated that about six million
boys were exposed to his films between 1936 and 1939.[47]
The most notorious combined entertainment and propaganda
film was Jud Süss which came out in 1940 and was a
great box office success. It was designed to foster
anti-Semitism. It catered for degraded tastes, with
rape and torture sequences, and its showing in Vienna
was followed by the trampling to death of an elderly
Jew on a public street, by a Hitler Youth band who had
seen the film.[48]

Best known of the propaganda films are Triumph

of the Will (1935) and Olympia (1938) by Leni Riefenstahl.
Controversy still rages over these, with conflicting
views of their artistry and iedological content, and
a back-handed tribute to the power of the first is
provided by opposition to its showing. As a piece of
education in the technique and content of Nazi propaganda
it can hardly be surpassed. It was meant as a show-
case of the Nuremberg rally, both at home and abroad.
In effect, it was to do visually what the radio could
do aurally. Nevertheless, despite, or perhaps because
of, its artistry, it was not a box office success. It
seems to have had limited appeal and a condensed
version about one-third of the original length was
usually shown. Moreover, though it won a prize in
France, only a few countries abroad friendly to Germany
showed it.[49]

These are the obvious mass media used to spread
Nazi propaganda, but the range of the Propaganda
Ministry's activity, as shown above, indicates how
widely it pervaded every aspect of cultural and
intellectual life. Censorship applied not only to
the press and film but also to the stage and literature.
There were book burnings and purgings of libraries.
The Nazis had their official art, very representational,
in which nature, peasant and family motifs abounded.
They castigated all else, for example in the exhibitions
of Degenerate Art. Even the applied arts were used
to spread the Nazi message. Propaganda pervaded every
aspect of public and private life.

Above all they were anxious that no individual
should find support and cohesion in any group not
permeated with their spirit. To this end, they broke
up or took over all other clubs and associations,
whether economic, business, trade union, religious,
special interest or purely social. This process as
it affected one German town is vividly described by
W. S. Allen in a chapter which he aptly calls 'The
Atomization of Society'. He concludes:

    Thus by the summer of 1933, the Nazis had either
    broken up, altered, fused, or brought under

control most of the clubs and societies of
Thalburg. The complex and diversified social
organization of the town had been almost completely
uprooted. In most cases the Nazis tried to fill
the vacuum, but often people stopped coming
altogether. . . . What social life there was
continued in the most basic gatherings: the
Stammtisch, the beer-and-cards evenings, or small
social gatherings in homes. Even these were
threatened as people began to distrust one another.
What was the value of getting together with
others to talk if you had to be careful about
what you said? Thus to a great extent the
individual was atomized. By the process of
Gleichschaltung [variously translated as
standardization, or putting everything in the
same gear] individuals had no choice: solitude
or mass relationships via some Nazi organization.[50]

Mention has already been made of one of the earliest
organizations which the Nazis intended to act as
replacements: the Hitler Youth. Like all dictators,
Hitler set great store by capturing the next generation.
In a speech on 6 November 1933 he said: 'When an
opponent declares, "I will not come over to your side",
I calmly say, "Your child belongs to us already. . . .
What are you? You will pass on. Your descendants,
however, now stand in the new camp. In a short time,
they will know nothing but this community."'[51]
Obviously Nazi propaganda permeated the educational
system totally, but they also took over most of the
out of school hours of youth as well. As we have
seen above, there was a natural appeal to youth in
the movement, but even so, at the beginning of 1933
it had only 1% of the total membership of youth
organizations in the country. At first pressure was
used to make others join, but in December 1936 all
German Youth had to join.[52] This captive membership was
then thoroughly propagandized. After 1934 a monthly
Film Hour was mandatory in all groups.[53] The programme
for a fortnight's camp,[54] with its daily patriotic pass-
word, propagandist motto, and ideological discussion
subject for the community hour, shows how they were
saturated with propaganda.

The other movement which drew vast numbers of
workers was 'Strength Through Joy', created in 1933
to help the worker to use leisure hours profitably.
It concerned itself with securing attendance at
lectures, concerts, theatres, opera and sports
activities. It operated travel schemes, enabling workers
to spend holidays abroad, and even made plans for the
Volkswagen, the people's car. It was also closely
associated with radio programming of a cultural and
uplifting nature.

Finally, in this necessarily incomplete survey
of propaganda methods, there was the greatest show-
case of all, both for domestic and foreign audiences:
the Nuremberg Rallies. These, where all Hitler's
propaganda ideas from Mein Kampf could be brought
into play, became ever more grandiose. As soon as
the Nazis seized power Hitler began the building of
a colossal permanent setting for the rallies, which
was intended to become the centre of the cultic
tradition of the Thousand Year Reich. Building continued
even into the war, and it was so dear to Hitler's
heart that it was not stopped until 1943. Everything
was planned to be on a massive scale, the site covering
an area of 16.5 square kilometres. The military parade
ground was to seat 160,000, and to have a platform for
important visitors, crowned with a sculpture 46 feet
higher than the Statue of Liberty. A huge stadium
was planned which would seat 400,000 spectators.[55]
Hitler justified this grandiose conception thus, in
a speech in 1939: 'I do this to restore to each
individual German his self-respect. In a hundred areas
I want to say to the individual: we are not inferior;
on the contrary we are the complete equal of every
other nation.'[56]

Every rally was conceived in stage and operatic
terms, as is shown by the system of markers on the
parade ground for the exact distribution of the 8,000
banners; the enormous number of spotlights and klieg
lights; and the control panel of coloured lights Hitler
had in front of him.[57] Triumph of the Will gives a
clear idea of the massed power, the sense of solidarity,

and the quasi-religious feeling that could be induced
by the events of these rallies. Lest this should be
seen as the distorting lens of Leni Riefenstahl, I
will quote two more neutral accounts of the powerful
impact the rallies made. The New York Times reporter
wrote:

> As he [Hitler] appeared there shone upward from
> a hidden circle of 150 army searchlights behind
> the grandstands as many spears of light to the
> central point above. It was the same device
> employed at the closing ceremony of the Olympic
> Games but it was greatly improved and enlarged. . . .
> Then suddenly there appeared in the distance
> a mass of advancing red colour. It was the
> 25,000 banners of Nazi organizations from all
> parts of Germany . . . there was presented a
> spectacle of a great tide of crimson seeping
> through the lanes between the solid blocs of
> brown. Simultaneously the minor searchlights
> along the pillared rim above the grandstands
> were turned down on the field, lighting up
> the gilded eagles on the standards, so the
> flood of red was flecked with gold. The effect
> was indescribably beautiful.[58]

The second quotation is from Sir Nevile Henderson,
the British Ambassador to Germany, who described a
Nuremberg rally thus: 'I had spent six years in St.
Petersburg before the war in the best days of the old
Russian ballet but for grandiose beauty I have never
seen a ballet to compare with it.'[59]

Above all the rallies were participatory functions
with choric speaking to enhance the sense of solidarity,
and fervid shouts of Sieg Heil. The New York Times
reporter recounts the extraordinary effect produced
when the closing ceremony was relayed to a hotel lounge
filled with working journalists, from foreign countries
and, one would have thought, hard-bitten and resistant:

> As the cheers from the hall following the 'Sieg
> Heil' with which he concluded died away, the hotel

audience to a man and woman rose to its feet
with arms raised in the Nazi salute and joined
in the emotional singing of 'Deutschland' followed
by the 'Horst Wessel Lied'. It was typical of
eight days of steadily mounting excitement that
words fail adequately to describe.[60]

This massed power and mounting excitement were conveyed
across Germany and the world by radio, film and press.

Section III: Some Questions and Conclusions

Such were the main outlines of the propaganda
system created by the Nazis. Apart from viewing it
with awe and horror, we have, I think, by way of
conclusion, to consider three inter-related questions.
How far could it succeed against the people's will,
and therefore what was the extent of its success? Was
it a means or an end? Did it contain the seeds of its
own destruction? These are large questions which can
only be touched on briefly here.

To start with the first question, it is obvious
that the propagandees must place themselves in a position
to be receptive: they must look at the poster; buy and
read the papers; attend the cinema or meeting; switch
on and listen to the radio. As we have seen above,
the propaganda machine did everything it could to ensure
that they had no choice. This was particularly true
of the use of radio and of the indoctrination of children
at school and youth organizations. But even more, the
propagandees must be psychologically receptive to the
ideas presented. Goebbels realized this when he was
careful to ensure that specific propaganda was directed
to specific groups, and Hitler even more so when he
spoke of the 'living corrective' of the audience. To
some extent they were drawing out what was already
there. Albert Speer, in looking back on his own first
experience of Hitler's speeches, writes, 'As I see it
today, these politicians in particular were in fact
moulded by the mob itself, guided by its yearnings
and its daydreams. . . . Certainly the masses roared to

the beat set by Hitler's and Goebbels's baton; yet they were not the true conductors. The mob determined the theme.'[61] A recent German writer has described propaganda as 'not only a means of manipulation but an indicator of what people sincerely hoped to be true.'[62] A similar view is taken by Jacques Ellul, who, in denying that the process of propagandizing involves an active (evil) element and a passive (victim) element, describes it as 'a sociological phenomenon in the sense that it has roots and reasons in the needs of the group that will sustain it'.[63]

There can be no denying that many Germans of this period craved leadership, authority, a sense of direction, a strong nationalist, and even militarist, government. Many people felt the attraction of a movement which called for a sense of sacrifice and offered them through this, and through commitment to what seemed a larger cause, a chance of reintegration into a community, and, supposedly, a classless community. Nazi propaganda could build on all these desires. It could build on patriotism, on the desire to be recognized as a great Power again, and to remove the humiliating features of the Treaty of Versailles. Ian Kershaw, in his challenge to the accepted view of the success of Nazi propaganda, distinguishes areas where propaganda could build on accepted values from those where a consensus had to be manufactured, or hostile counter-prevailing forces existed. He finds the chief success in the first category.[64] These accepted values, which I have listed above, coalesced in the creation of the Führer Myth, in the success of which as a unifying principle in the state, Goebbels took much pride. Significantly, as was pointed out at the beginning of this paper, this myth held to the end of the war, long past when reality should have destroyed it. The Führer was presented as above politics, and as personally responsible for the achievements of the 1930s, which had done so much to restore German pride. Up to 1939 propaganda operated against a background of considerable success: there was a series of achievements gained without bloodshed. And this is a significant point: the Führer was presented as a man of peace. The whole

tenor of Nazi propaganda glorified war and was designed
to prepare the nation for war, but in this it did not
succeed. There were no cheering crowds for war in
1939, as there had been in 1914.

The same qualification holds good with regard to
anti-Semitism: it was difficult for propaganda to succeed
where people had personal knowledge of Jewish people.
Kershaw considers the greatest success of propaganda
in this field to be in persuading people that there
was a Jewish question, and in depersonalizing the Jews,
but that terror and legal discrimination, not propaganda,
were behind the exclusion of Jews.[65] A recent study
of a small town in Germany records numerous small acts
of kindness to Jews, and would bear out the difficulty
of propagandizing people whose personal experience
contradicted the propaganda.[66] The Nazis tried to use
propaganda 'as a tool to destroy the disturbing
independence of reality',[67] but without entire success.
They did not have enough time to see if their methods
would have worked in the vacuum they tried to create
for the younger generation, as suggested in Hitler's
speech quoted above. But many of the soldiers who
continued the hopeless fight must have been indoctrinated
through the Hitler Youth. On the evidence above we
must conclude that the propaganda machine was most
successful where it articulated desires already present,
where the people willed their own fate, though without
fully understanding what they willed.

This brings us to the second question: was
propaganda a means or an end? It is hard to read
Mein Kampf without feeling that there is a blurring
of distinction between the two. There is so little
ideological content in this book. It is mainly a
diatribe of hate and destruction with the only positive
concept that of power, essentially for its own sake.
Even the few ideas seem shaped to the propaganda
methods that are so vividly described. Did Hitler's
obsessive hatred of the Jews lead him to see their
hand everywhere, or was it his propaganda concept of
the single foe? Did he really believe in the nation
as community, or was this his way of winning the masses?

It is difficult to see anything in this work but a total
disregard of people, as such, and a total glorification
of power. Every aspect of the propaganda machine that
this paper has examined seems ultimately devoid of
positive content but, rather, imbued with nihilism.
In a telling phrase Allen speaks of 'a ritual devoid
of inner content'.[68] Ellul has again pinpointed this
aspect of modern propaganda. Lenin and Hitler, he says,
were responsible for a great innovation.

> It was to understand that the modern world is
> essentially a world of means. . . . This completely
> transformed the relations between ideology and
> propaganda. . . . Propaganda then became the major
> fact; with respect to it, ideologies became mere
> epiphenomena. . . . Some will object that the great
> movements that have used propaganda, such as
> Communism or Nazism, did have a doctrine and did
> create an ideology. I reply that this was not
> their principal object: ideology and doctrine
> were merely accessories used by propaganda to
> mobilize individuals. The aim was the power of
> the party or State, supported by the masses.[69]

Certainly the evidence marshalled above would suggest
no fixed body of doctrine, but rather the determination
to articulate the desires of as many as possible, so
as to secure the integration of the individual in the
State, and thus a readiness for whatever policy the
State wished to carry out.

Finally, the third question: did Nazi propaganda
contain the seeds of its own destruction? I have
suggested above that it was self-defeating in many of
its forms. People ceased to buy papers; films lost
money; social organizations withered; standardization
struck at the cultural life of the nation, which, if
there was any point in the glorification of the Volk,
should have been flourishing. One could add that it
is considered the grip on ideas and education set back
German science and thus contributed to eventual defeat
in the war. Moreover, the central concept of the cult,
and the one it was most successful in projecting, the

leadership principle, was itself self-defeating. The
Führer myth, projecting Hitler as the Saviour sent by
God to Germany, was constantly emphasized in every
aspect of propaganda.[70] This image, built on early
successes, inevitably called for continuing successes
to sustain it, and thus encouraged the tendency already
present to take greater and greater risks, and to pursue
a more and more adventurous policy. This need for
constant success had other effects, it has been suggested,
in making Hitler reluctant to move too far in the
direction of a war economy, when war came. He opposed
rationing, and taxes remained relatively low. 'German
output of consumer goods was hardly dented by the war,
between 1939 and 1942.'[71] Thus, again, the needs of
propaganda hampered the success of the very objective
it was designed to serve.

Moreover, the creation of the Führer myth fostered
an impression of infallibility, isolating Hitler more
and more from any point of view but his own. The frenzy
of the crowds at meetings ended in Hitler hypnotizing
himself. 'The irrational adulation and deification
of Hitler demonstrated during this hysterical week
[Nuremberg Party rally, 1934] increased Hitler's
megalomania; he felt that he could now whip the German
masses into any frenzy, that they would carry out any
order he might give them.'[72] When there were no
successes to build on, and this reaction was less
likely to sustain him, Hitler withdrew from the public
eye, listened less and less to advice and became more
and more divorced from reality. In other words, the
aim of propaganda 'to destroy the disturbing independence
of reality'[67] was most successful on the propagandist
himself. How far propaganda was self-destructive in
this way is hard to determine, however, since the
indeterminant factor is the war. But war, as we have
seen above, was inherent in Nazi propaganda from the
start, and, as we have also seen, the needs of
propaganda themselves hindered the war effort in some
areas. The conclusion must be therefore that it
contained large self-destructive forces.

NOTES

1. Richard Taylor, 'Goebbels and the Function of Propaganda' in Nazi Propaganda: the Power and the Limitations, edited by David Welch (London, 1983), pp. 29-44 (p. 29).

2. Ian Kershaw, 'The Führer Image and Political Integration: the popular conception of Hitler in Bavaria during the Third Reich' in The Führer State: Myth and Reality (London, 1981), pp. 133-161.

3. Jacques Ellul, Propaganda (New York, 1966), p. 284, footnote, and p. 285.

4. Ellul, p. 61.

5. Quoted in Taylor, p. 36.

6. Adolf Hitler, Mein Kampf (Boston, 1943). All references, given in brackets in the text, are to this edition.

7. Alan Bullock, Hitler: a Study in Tyranny (Harmondsworth, 1962), p. 69.

8. Quoted in Bullock, p. 69.

9. Jeremy Noakes and Geoffrey Pridham, Documents on Nazism 1919-1945 (London, 1974), p. 340.

10. For example, there is a clear exposition of this idea in Hugh Dalziel Duncan, Communication and Social Order (London, 1962), pp. 238-248.

11. Duncan, in a footnote, p. 249, gives Hanfstaengl's account of the origin of this: 'I started playing some of the football marches I had picked up at Harvard. I explained to Hitler all the business about the cheer leaders and college songs and the deliberate whipping up of hysterical enthusiasm. I told him about the thousands of spectators being made to roar, "Harvard, Harvard, Harvard, rah, rah,

rah!" in unison and of the hypnotic effect of
this sort of thing. . . . I had Hitler fairly
shouting with enthusiasm. "That is it, Hanfstaengl,
that is what we need for the movement, marvelous",
and he pranced up and down the room like a drum
majorette . . ."Rah, rah, rah!" became "Sieg Heil,
Sieg Heil!" -that is the origin of it. . . .'

12. Oron J. Hale, <u>The Captive Press in the Third Reich</u>
    (Princeton, 1964), pp. 31 and 59.

13. Hale, p. 50.

14. Noakes and Pridham, pp. 103-104, and W. S. Allen,
    <u>The Nazi Seizure of Power</u> (New York, 1973), p. 72.

15. Allen, pp. 73-74.

16. Ernest K. Bramsted, <u>Goebbels and National Socialist
    Propaganda</u> (East Lansing, Michigan, 1965), p. 20.

17. Allen, pp. 46-64.

18. Allen, pp. 44 and 135.

19. William L. Shirer, <u>The Rise and Fall of the Third
    Reich</u> (New York, 1960), p. 252.

20. Allen, p. 73.

21. Noakes and Pridham, pp. 108-110, and Allen
    pp. 108-109.

22. Bramsted, pp. 23-31.

23. Hamilton T. Burden, <u>The Nuremberg Party Rallies
    1923-1939</u> (New York, 1967), pp. 38-45.

24. Z. A. B. Zeman, <u>Nazi Propaganda</u> (London, 1964),
    pp. 34-36, and Bullock pp. 200-201.

25. Some idea of this effect can be gained from Leni
    Riefenstahl's film, <u>The Triumph of the Will</u>, in

whose opening sequence shots of clouds, sunlight,
and the plane's shadow passing over the columns
of men manage to associate the ideas of the eagle
and the ancient gods.

26. G. L. Mosse, Nazi Culture (New York, 1966), pp.
    291-293.

27. Bullock, pp. 217, 230 and 238.

28. Noakes and Pridham, p. 331.

29. Harwood L. Childs, editor, Propaganda and
    Dictatorship (Princeton, 1936), pp. 19-20.

30. Hale, p. 82.

31. Hale, p. 121.

32. Quoted in Hale, p. 155.

33. Hale, p. 267.

34. The editor of the Völkischer Beobachter in a 1948
    interview, quoted in Hale, p. 246.

35. Hale, p. 323.

36. Hale, p. 232.

37. Walter B. Emery, National and International Systems
    of Broadcasting (East Lansing, Michigan, 1969),
    pp. 296-298.

38. Bramsted, p. 74.

39. Thomas Grandin, The Political Use of Radio (Geneva
    Studies, vol. 10, No. 3, August 1939), p. 14 and
    for a detailed account of one such occurrence,
    Allen, p. 244.

40. Grandin, p. 13.

41. Serge Chakotin, The Rape of the Masses (New York, 1940), p. 93.

42. Marshall McLuhan, Understanding Media: the Extensions of Man (New York, 1964). In this controversial book, Marshall McLuhan devotes a chapter ('Radio: the Tribal Drum') to radio and makes the claim 'That Hitler came into political existence at all is directly owing to radio and public address systems' (p. 300).

43. Taylor, p. 40.

44. David Welch, Propaganda and the German Cinema 1933-1945) (Oxford, 1983), p. 311.

45. David Stewart Hull, Film in the Third Reich (Berkeley, California, 1969), p. 36.

46. Hull, p. 8.

47. Hull, pp. 118-119.

48. Hull, p. 169.

49. Burden, pp. 97-98.

50. Allen, ch. 14 and, in particular, pp. 225-226.

51. Quoted in Shirer, p. 249.

52. Noakes and Pridham, pp. 353-356.

53. Hull, p. 51.

54. Noakes and Pridham, pp. 358-361.

55. Albert Speer, Inside the Third Reich (New York, 1971), pp. 107-108.

56. Quoted in Speer, p. 109.

57. Burden, pp. 60-63.

58. New York Times, 12 September 1936, quoted in Burden, p. 128.

59. Quoted in Welch, Film, p. 159.

60. New York Times, 15 September 1937, quoted in Burden p. 146.

61. Speer, pp. 45–46.

62. Lothar Kettenacker, 'Sozialpsychologishe Aspekte der Führer Herrschaft' in The Führer State: Myth and Reality: Politics of the Third Reich (London, 1981), pp. 98–131, English Summary pp. 131–132 (p. 131).

63. Ellul, p. 121.

64. Ian Kershaw, 'How Effective was Nazi Propaganda?' in David Welch Nazi Propaganda: the Power and the Limitations (London, 1983), pp. 180–201.

65. Kershaw, How Effective, p. 191.

66. Sabina Lietzman, 'Daily Life in the Third Reich', review of Victims and Neighbors: A Small Town in Nazi Germany Remembered by Frances Henry, in The New York Times Book Review (28 October 1984), p. 38.

67. Siegfried Kracauer, From Calgari to Hitler: a Psychological History of the German Film (Princeton 1947), p. 295.

68. Allen, p. 245.

69. Ellul, pp. 195–197.

70. Joachim Remak, editor, The Nazi Years (Englewood Cliffs, New Jersey, 1969), p. 69, for example, but many other examples could be quoted.

71. Norman Stone, Hitler (London, 1980), p. 123.

72. Burden, p. 91.

73. Bramsted, pp. 224–227. In the winter of 1942–3
    Hitler spoke in public only once, and, after
    that, there were only two more public speeches
    and two funeral addresses. From 1943–4 there
    were only three radio speeches.

BIBLIOGRAPHY

Allen, William Sheridan. The Nazi Seizure of Power.
    New York, 1973.

Barsam, Richard Meran. Filmguide to 'Triumph of the
    Will'. Bloomington, Indiana, 1975.

Bessel, Richard. 'Living with the Nazis: Some recent
    writing on the Social History of the Third
    Reich', review article in European History
    Quarterly, Vol. 14 (1984), pp. 211-220.

Bramsted, Ernest K. Goebbels and National Socialist
    Propaganda 1925-1945. East Lansing, Michigan,
    1965.

------------. 'The Do's and Don'ts of Goebbels',
    review of Politik der Tauschungen by Fritz
    Sanger. The Times Literary Supplement, 18 June
    1976, p. 737.

Bullock, Alan. Hitler: a Study in Tyranny. Harmondsworth
    1962.

Burden, Hamilton T. The Nuremberg Party Rallies
    1923-1939. New York, 1967.

Chakotin, Serge. The Rape of the Masses. New York,
    1940.

Childs, Harold L., editor. Propaganda and Dictatorship.
    Princeton, 1936.

Doob, Leonard W. 'Goebbels' Principles of Propaganda'
    in Public Opinion and Propaganda by Daniel Katz
    and others. New York, 1954.

Duncan, Hugh Dalziel. Communication and Social Order.
    London, 1962.

Ellul, Jacques. Propaganda. New York, 1966.

Emery Walter B. National and International Systems of Broadcasting. East Lansing, Michigan, 1969.

Gannon, Franklin Reid. The British Press and Germany. Oxford, 1971.

German Historical Institute. The Führer State : Myth and Reality Studies in the Structure and Politics of the Third Reich. Publications of the German Historical Institute, vol. 8. London, 1981.

Grandin, Thomas. The Political Use of Radio. Geneva Studies, vol. 10, No. 3, August 1939.

Hale, Oron J. The Captive Press in the Third Reich Princeton, 1964.

Hitler, Adolf. Mein Kampf. Boston, 1943.

Hull, David Stewart. Film in the Third Reich. Berkeley, California, 1969.

Kracauer, Siegfried. From Calgari to Hitler: a Psychological History of the German Film. Princeton, 1947.

Lietzmann, Sabina. 'Daily Life in the Third Reich', review of Victims and Neighbors: A Small Town in Nazi Germany Remembered by Frances Henry. The New York Times Book Review, 28 October 1984, p. 38.

McLuhan, Marshall. Understanding Media: The Extensions of Man. New York, 1964.

Manvell, Roger and Heinrich Fraenkel. The German Cinema. New York, 1971.

Mosse, G. L. Nazi Culture. New York, 1966.

Noakes, Jeremy and Geoffrey Pridham. Documents on Nazism 1919-1945. London, 1974.

Remak, Joachim, editor. The Nazi Years. Englewood
    Cliffs, New Jersey, 1969.

Shirer, William L. The Rise and Fall of the Third
    Reich. New York, 1960.

Speer, Albert. Inside the Third Reich. New York, 1971.

Stone, Norman. Hitler. London, 1980.

Trevor-Roper, H. R. The Last Days of Hitler. New York,
    1947.

Welch, David, editor. Nazi Propaganda: the Power and
    the Limitations. London, 1983.

-------------. Propaganda and the German Cinema
    1933-1945. Oxford, 1983.

Zeman, Z. A. B. Nazi Propaganda. London, 1964.

CHAPTER 7

Some Errors to Avoid

In this final chapter I do not propose to break new ground. The points raised have for the most part been dealt with, at least implicitly, in the preceding chapters, Nevertheless, it is, I feel, valuable to recapitulate the main varieties of error in student papers. My approach is not theoretic, but purely practical. I do not attempt to survey the major danger areas. This chapter is, quite simply, the record of what I have found to be the most frequently committed blunders.

I group my remarks under four heads: Purpose and Conclusion; Documentation; Shape and Flow; Presentation.

Purpose and Conclusion

(a) A research paper should be circular in argument. That is, the formal aim of the paper should be stated in the opening paragraph; the conclusion should return to the opening, and examine the original purpose in the light of the data assembled. It is a prime error to present conclusions that are not directly related to the evidence previously presented. For example, a student paper entitled 'The Significance of Freud' reached, after an examination of Freud's thinking, the following conclusion: 'Because of the application and acceptance of his theories, Sigmund Freud has had a greater influence on both scientific and popular thought and belief than any other psychologist or physician of the past century.' Now this statement may be perfectly true, but as a conclusion it will not stand up. The *title* implies at least a look at Freud's disciples, revisers and opponents. This, in the paper cited, was not performed. The *conclusion* fits the title well enough, but not the body of the paper. The writer was not in a position, on the evidence he had marshalled, to arrive at the conclusion which he did. The student had clearly reverted to the title in making his conclusion without reference to what his paper had actually said.

Now we have to be pragmatic about this. In a strict laboratory sense, it is necessary to lay down *at the start* of the research the aims and methods. The data and conclusions then follow. But in a less rigorously scientific context, one often starts the research with no more than a sense of direction, and pursues it until a pattern emerges. This pattern will then determine the purpose, which is stated at the opening, and this in turn is pursued to the conclusion. The great failure is not to review the work at the end, and not to ensure that the sequence of purpose, data, conclusions forms a consistent and co-ordinated whole.

(b) A further aspect of purpose should be mentioned. A writer should have a clear idea of the audience to whom the paper is addressed. Is it lay, or specialist? The question is important, because on the answer will turn the inclusion of much subsidiary material. It is easy both to over-emphasize and under-emphasize the amount of specialized, technical knowledge (and jargon) to be included in a paper. If the subject demands the inclusion of technical terms, a small glossary may be added to the paper. If the subject is of the humanities, but demanding a constant reference to obscure facts, the writer has to consider well how much can be expected of the reader. Even a Professor of History, say, might like to be reminded of the name and office of one of the minor members of Chamberlain's National Government. On the other hand, experts find it extraordinarily irritating to be bombarded with minor information that they are perfectly aware of. The whole question needs to be thought out very carefully. The crime is not to ponder the question: 'For whom am I writing?'

Documentation

(a) This area I unhesitatingly nominate as having the chief concentration of student failings in the writing of research papers. I need not labour the commoner failings: lack of dates, lack of author's initials, lack of.the full details required for documentation. These failings may be ascribed to sloth; as may the simple reluctance to footnote at all. I do not inveigh against sloth; I merely point out that work produced with such disregard for the principle of documentation cannot be dignified with the title of 'Research Paper'. But these are gross crimes. They are worse than crimes: blunders. To claim a large Bibliography (without having made use of it), however, cannot be readily detected, and this must be termed a sin. I can only recommend researchers to set down, in their Bibliographies, no more than may rightfully be claimed. They may be questioned on the sources by their instructors, but essentially the matter remains a private one — between themselves and the Muse of Scholarship.

(b) As sinful, but more readily detected, is the tendency to pass off a direct quotation as one's own sentence — presumably, to avoid the tedium of appending a footnote. Since sloth is by no means to be correlated with intelligence, it is interesting to observe that writers guilty of this fault quite often carry it out inefficiently. A sudden change of style can be quite easily detected by a perceptive reader. It is not difficult to guess the truth in the following extract: 'What's wrong with advertising? I do not see that the critics have such a good case. It is not clear how far the widespread anxiety and hostility among the intellectual, literary and cultural critics of advertising is shared by the general public. Further, it is not clear how far the fears that advertising inculcates wrong values and habits are supported by evidence.' No great literary gifts are needed to perceive that the first two and last two sentences in this extract are written by different people. The colloquial, decidedly non-literary phrasing of the first part contrasts painfully with the careful, mandarin-type prose of the second. That is why I regard such a practice as unintelligent. Not all styles contrast so obviously; but instructors easily acquire the knack of spotting a word, a phrase, a sentence that is not in key with the rest of the paper. And the effort required to dovetail styles could more easily be directed to inserting quotation marks, and setting down a footnote.

(c) Even sound and conscientious students, who would not dream of concealing a direct quotation, are sometimes blind to the demands of footnoting. It is *not* sufficient to paraphrase all sources, and write up the paper, in one's own words, devoid of footnotes. The Bibliography lists all the sources used, but cannot relate them to the specific points in the paper. Where controversial matters are concerned, it is more than ever important to know *which* authorities are making the point. A paper on the Schlieffen plan, for example, can make a point far more tellingly if it relates this point to Gerhard Ritter, a modern German historian, and does not leave the point to be vaguely associated with an English historian of the 1920s. The whole value of the paper depends on the precise identification of each source used in the argument. One can say, then, that it is a quite basic failing to neglect this identification at all key points.

(d) A final weakness in this department is the inadequacy of the sources cited. Perhaps three important types of inadequacy may be discerned.

1. First, the sources may be out of date. One may say dogmatically that all Bibliographies should contain several sources published for the first time in the decade before the paper was written. And, however classic their stature, there are few works published before, say, 1970, that do not stand in some need of revision. Such works may be leaned on heavily, but not trusted absolutely. They should be checked against later works, articles and critical reviews. Students should be careful to check the scholarly journals related to their fields, at least for the few preceding years, to ensure that they know of all recent work that has been done in these fields. It is essential to avoid being asked by one's examiner or instructor, 'But were you not aware of the book/article recently published by Professor X?'

However decisive the influence of a seminal work such as Burckhardt's *The Civilization of the Renaissance in Italy* (1860) may be, it is folly to regard it as the epitome of modern thinking on the Renaissance. Even much more recent seminal works stand in some need of being reconsidered. The student should be aware that scholars have invested heavily in change.

2. Second, there is the inadequacy of one-sidedness. This is fatally easy to yield to. Some writers have become influential because they write well; others because they write badly. It is easy to fall under the spell of Macaulay's view of events, because he writes so well. It is easy to accept the ideas of Hegel or Dewey, because they are so hard to read. However they are cast, researchers should coldly resist all spells. They ought to aim at a spread of authorities. Especially they ought to remember that certain subjects are under quite fundamental attacks. They cannot, for example, regard psychoanalysis as a territory owned communally in perpetuity, and disputed over by Freudians, Adlerians, Stekelites, and so on. They should bear in mind that it is perfectly possible to dismiss psychoanalysis as an aberration in the history of psychology. The root failure in this category is perhaps a superstitious reverence for all manifestations of the printed word.

3. Third, many authorities are simply inadequate in themselves. They are lightweight, unreliable, obviously biased. To this category belong a variety of articles in the popular press; unsupported and possibly garbled news reports; statements on national policy culled from party political manifestoes; puffs and pamphlets; certain works published under the stresses of wartime pressures; works which are openly and blatantly confined to the grinding of a single axe. Such material, the biased and the trivial, may have a useful supporting role to play. No serious paper could be written around it as major sources.

Shape and Flow

(a) The aerodynamic shape, as it were, of the paper I have discussed in Chapter 4. A desirable shape is one in which the *natural form* of the topic has been discerned, and exploited. Failure to do this results in a paper that is as shapely as a sack or an amoeba. I find in practice two main varieties of this deformed shape. In the first variety, the basic structure is sound; but the treatment of a certain part of the paper may be over- or under-done. The bulkiness of a single part of the paper makes the whole work lop-sided; equally, a comparatively skimpy treatment leaves the reader frustrated and dissatisfied. Particularly is this true of topics with a historical basis. The researcher tends in the enthusiastic early phase to stockpile a mass of notes; the later periods may be less exhaustively treated. The second variety of shapelessness concerns the inclusion of a side issue. Sometimes the most eager researchers are guilty of this fault. They find themselves fascinated by an issue worth no more than a brief mention in the paper as a whole; devote considerable pains to covering the issue; and do not have the hardihood to excise this fascinating but irrelevant material. I repeat a warning I have given earlier: much, quite often most, research is *wasted*. One has to bear with this, and be ready to cut. To pursue the anatomical metaphor further, a paper should have a good bone-structure — and a good visual shape.

(b) On flow, I draw the reader's attention to the remarks on pages 46-7. Absence of flow indicates a stammering, disjointed paper. Apart from the guide words ('however', 'secondly', and so on) which I have recommended, I should like to emphasize the value of headings. A paper which is divided into anonymous 'Sections' and 'Chapters' is much harder to follow than one with descriptive headings. The reader ought to be told exactly what is coming up. Moreover, one can make the mental adjustment far more easily if the eye is helped by spacings, underlinings, use of different coloured inks, and other aids. A little imagination in the exploitation of typographic resources makes a quite amazing difference to the reader's ready comprehension of a paper. Finally, the writer ought if possible to make transitions easy, by referring in the first sentence of a new section to the position arrived at in the previous section.

Presentation

Few, if any, products sell well unless they are seductively packaged. That is a blunt fact of modern life which it is useless to decry, and still more to ignore. A quite astonishing number of students, in my experience, view the matter differently. They are disposed to the view that native worth, untrammelled by conventional presentation, is all. They are apt to regard conventional documentation, format, proofreading, and even spelling, as in some way a betrayal of their integrity. With this viewpoint I have no desire to undertake a laboured disputation. There are perhaps two points to be made. First, courtesy to one's readers suggests that one make their task as easy as possible. Second, the plainest self-interest demands that one's work be presented in the best possible light. Most of us, I imagine, know the feeling of drafting a passage in longhand — which we think to be not very good — and after typing out the draft, revising our opinion upwards. Essentially the same work looks far better. It is impossible to evade the consequences of this psychological fact. I can see no point whatsoever in neglecting this simple logic: if the world judges by appearances, let the appearances be on one's side.

In practice this has two important implications. Care has to be devoted to the visual techniques of presentation: decent margins, ample spacings, well-judged headings, appropriate underlinings. Then, proofreading should be absolute. This is the worst single chore an author has to tackle. There is no escape at all, but I strongly recommend that a friend be induced, on a treaty of reciprocity, to duplicate one's proofreading. The eye has a quite amazing capacity to miss the identical error a dozen times running. A fresh eye spots it immediately. It is worth the labour. The sense of irritation which a reader experiences when encountering an otherwise excellent work whose appearance is ruined by shoddy proofreading is not easily to be described. I have before me a major work, brought out by a reputable publisher, which contains three gross errors on the opening page. It is hard to see the labour of months let down badly for want of half an hour's concentrated proofreading at the end.

There is one final point to make. The basic virtue of research is accuracy. And for this virtue nobody's memory is sufficient; nobody's care in copying quotations is sufficient. Therefore, let all quotations be checked at the last. I end with the advice of Dr. Routh — all wisdom consists of truisms: 'You will find it a very good practice always to verify your references, Sir!'

CHAPTER 8

Publication in a Learned Journal

At some point the researcher may wish to publish findings in a learned journal. Characteristically, this will be a matter of preparing a chapter in a thesis or dissertation for publication. The essential guidance and scholarly confirmation have already been provided by the supervisors. It is now up to the researcher. How does one make the transition from academic exercise to published work?

What follows is direct advice. I assume that the reader is in no doubt as to the professional desirability of a wider audience, and of placing a publication on the permanent record. This is how it is done.

1. The first point to grasp is the unsuitability of thesis material in its original form. Editors and publishers loathe theses. That is because they tend to be written in a style too cumbersome for the professional reading public. Theses are written for supervisors who have to be convinced that one has really done the work. No corners are cut. Space is no object. I once remarked to a PhD candidate at his defence of a dissertation on *Macbeth*, 'Enjoy it. This is the last time in your life you will get away with writing 600 pages on a single play.' Nothing of this applies to learned journals. Among other things, Editors care about space and footnotes; they have to cost the printers' bills. They also want to reduce the sawdust factor permissible in theses. The idea that publishing is simply a matter of retyping a thesis chapter, with renumbered pages and a few minor changes, will not long survive in the real world. The material will have to be rethought and rewritten.

2. The professional reading public, for whom the material is reworked, is highly sophisticated. It doesn't need to have everything spelled out. The writer will have to produce credentials, but need not overwhelm the readers with a parade of footnotes. A culling operation among the lesser footnotes is in order, and the major footnotes ought to imply each other. The professional reading public would like to learn something it did not already know, expressed in succinct prose, the points made in an agile and alert manner. Hence, the writer should think of presenting work that is altogether more *taut* than the original exercise. The fat is shed. What is left is muscle.

3. The great rule is: TARGET THE JOURNAL. It is useless to think,

in a general way, of 'preparing work for publication'. That phrase is meaningless. Publication in what? Journals are not interchangeable, and Editors are rightly proud of the identity and individuality of their journals. They expect writers to study form for the course, and will give short shrift to those who fail blatantly. They are alert to the novice's error of mailing a paper without regard to the character of the journal. That error guarantees a speedy match of MS to SAE. It is no good thinking vaguely of publishing in sociology, aesthetics, history. The specific journal is everything: *New Statesman and Society, History Today*. How does the *British Journal of Aesthetics* rate against the *Journal of Aesthetics and Art Criticism*?

4. Hence, the companion rule is: RESEARCH THE MARKET. The writer should confront the question: How well do you know the available journals in your field? Of course one browses among the open shelves of the library, but unless it is exceptionally well served it can hardly subscribe to all the well-regarded journals in the field. The number of available journals is really enormous. The writer would be well advised to turn back to Chapter 1, Bibliography Section, page 14, where there is general guidance on the various guides to learned journals. In addition, those working in a literary field might like to look at *The Times Literary Supplement* for 22 November 1985, a special issue containing a wide spread of advertisements for literary journals. Language is not necessarily a barrier; certain foreign journals will publish some articles in English. A given article in English might well appear in *Shakespeare Jahrbuch*, or *Cahiers Elisabéthains*, or *Studia Anglia Posnaniensa*.

Then again, research may be of interest to a journal of broader concern than one's own specialist area. Can the material be shaped towards a larger academic or general public? The titles of many well-respected journals give no direct clue as to their contents. North American colleges and universities have a number of excellent journals hospitable to well-written pieces of interest to the general academic community — *Kenyon Review, Sewanee Review, Virginia Quarterly Review* and so on. There is no quick way of sizing them up. One has to browse through past issues to get an idea of form.

Even in a narrow academic sense, material may be presented from several aspects. Suppose one locates some unpublished letters of G. B. Shaw: the obvious journal is *Shaw Review*. But the letters might bear upon the theatre, upon public life, upon the Fabian Society. Each of these areas implies its own range of interested journals. In the humanities, one should not have hard-and-fast ideas about the 'appropriate' outlet. A certain flexibility and receptivity to new categories is desirable.

5. One draws up a short list, and then targets the first journal on the list. From now on all efforts are directed to placing an article in that journal. My advice is as follows.

(i) The selection of the targeted journal precedes the drafting of the paper. Before beginning the draft, immerse yourself in the journal at which you aim. Try to soak up its characteristics. What is its preferred length? Does it favour the blockbuster footnote 1, which sums up all previous research on the subject, or does it prefer a more muted style of documentation? Is your topic well within its range? Should it be cut down, or expanded?

(ii) If you are in doubt, it is perfectly in order to write a preliminary letter to the Editor, enclosing an abstract of, say, 200 words on the article you have in mind, and asking if it would be welcome. Ideally, the Editor might reply indicating that 2,000 words on the topic would be of interest and would be considered. You then go ahead, working to whatever guidelines have been offered. If the answer is negative, you still have used your time profitably and must now repeat the process with another journal.

(iii) The great principle, for one unused to publication, is that the market speaking through the Editor takes over. Your personal impulses, wishes, idiosyncrasies will have to be restrained. Your prose will in any case be tailored to the house style, if nothing else; your views on the comma in adjectival sequences, for example, will be disregarded. It is the lot of authors.

(iv) The preferred style today is light, dry, crisp. That may not always be apparent in what one reads, but it is the style to aim for. The only advice my first Editor gave me was 'Be concise. Not short, but concise.' That still holds as good advice. The vices are pretentiousness and prolixity. Tone of voice is exceptionally difficult, but must be striven for; the reading public is composed of academic peers. For a general manual of prose style, I warmly recommend F. L. Lucas's *Style* and Sir Ernest Gowers' *Plain Words*. There is still no better crash course in English than George Orwell's essay 'Politics and the English Language'. Always the watchwords are clarity and simplicity.

(v) In presentation, follow the model of an article in the targeted journal, observing its footnote conventions. Do it the way the journal does: if the house style runs to full details of publication (Cambridge: Cambridge University Press, 1982), that is the way you do it. You can retype the notes for a resubmission. The article itself must be submitted on A4 paper with wide margins and double spacing. Read carefully what the Editors say, on the masthead pages, about submisssion of MSS. If they want SAEs or International Reply Coupons, so be it. Unless stated otherwise, the Editor will expect to receive the top copy of the MS submitted; you should keep the xerox yourself. If the MS is returned in a dog-eared state, retype it before the next submission. Editors lost their innocence a long time back, but they still like to receive a MS in pristine condition, that looks as if this is its first outing. Almost invariably the name of the Editor will be known, and stated on the masthead. The covering letter should be addressed to the Editor by name, following the principle that everyone likes to be identified as a human being as well as a functionary. Unless it is desirable to explain some circumstances of the research, it is unnecessary to make a prolonged business of the covering letter. A simple form of words suffices: 'Dear ----, I wish to submit the enclosed article ------ to your consideration, for publication in your journal.'

What Editors hope for is quality of research and writing allied to an intelligent and thoughtful attempt to conform to the character of their journals. The successful approach is based on the proposition: this will suit your journal.

Guidelines for Nonsexist Language in APA Journals

The *Publication Manual* of the American Psychological Association (1974, p. 28) suggests that journal authors 'be aware of the current move to avoid generic use of male nouns and pronouns when content refers to both sexes . . . [and] avoid overuse of the pronoun *he* when *she* or *they* is equally appropriate'. The first change sheet to the *Publication Manual* (1975, p. 2) says: 'For some specific suggestions on how to avoid such language, see "Guidelines for Nonsexist Use of Language", which was prepared by the APA Task Force on Issues of Sexual Bias in Graduate Education and published in the June 1975 *American Psychologist* (pp. 682–684).' Those guidelines, while helpful, are not specific to journal articles.

This second change sheet states the policy on sexist language in APA journals, offers some general principles for journal authors to consider, and suggests some ways to avoid sexist language.

To obtain single copies of this change sheet, send a stamped, self-addressed envelope to Publication Manual, Change Sheet 2, American Psychological Association, 1200 Seventeenth Street, N.W., Washington, D.C. 20036.

Policy Statement

APA as a publisher accepts journal authors' word choices unless those choices are inaccurate, unclear or ungrammatical. However, because APA as an organization is committed to both science and the fair treatment of individuals and groups, authors of journal articles are expected to avoid writing in a manner that reinforces questionable attitudes and assumptions about people and sex roles.

Language that reinforces sexism can spring from subtle errors in research design, inaccurate interpretation, or imprecise word choices. Faulty logic in design, for example, may lead an investigator to report sex differences when the stimulus materials and measures used give one sex an unwarranted advantage over the other. Or, in interpretation, and investigator may make unwarranted generalizations about all people from data about one sex. Imprecise word choices, which occur frequently in journal writing, may be interpreted as biased, discriminatory, or demeaning even if they are not intended to be.

Advice on research design and interpretation is beyond the scope of the APA *Publication Manual*. However, in the spirit of the guidelines on writing style in Chapter 2, the following guidelines on nonsexist language are intended to help authors recognize and change instances where word choices may be inaccurate, misleading, or discriminatory.

Guidelines

Sexism in journal writing may be classified into two categories that are conceptually different: problems of *designation* and problems of *evaluation*.

Problems of Designation

An author must use care in choosing words to ensure accuracy, clarity, and freedom from bias. In the case of sexism, long-established cultural practice can exert a powerful insidious influence over even the most conscientious author. Nouns, pronouns, and adjectives that designate persons can be chosen to eliminate, or at least to minimize the possibility of ambiguity in sex identity or sex role. In the following examples, problems of designation are divided into two subcategories: *ambiguity of referent*, where it is unclear whether the author means one or both sexes, and *stereotyping*, where the writing conveys unsupported or biased connotations about sex roles and identity.

Problems of Evaluation

By definition, scientific writing should be free of implied or irrelevant evaluation of the sexes. Difficulties may derive from the habitual use of clichés, or familiar expressions, such as 'man and wife'. The use of *man and wife* together implies differences in the freedom and activities of each, and evaluation of roles can occur. Thus, *husband and wife* are parallel, *man and wife* are not. In the examples that follow, problems of evaluation, like problems of designation, are divided into *ambiguity of referent* and *sterotyping*.

I. *Problems of Designation*

Examples of common usage	Consider meaning. An alternative may be better	Comment
	A. *Ambiguity of Referent*	
1. The *client* is usually the best judge of the value of *his* counseling.	The *client* is usually the best judge of the value of counseling.	*His* deleted.

Examples of common usage	Consider meaning. An alternative may be better.	Comment
	Clients are usually the best judges of the value of the counseling they receive.	Changed to plural.
	The best judge of the value of counseling is usually *the client*.	Rephrased.
2. *Man's search* for knowledge has led *him* into ways of learning that bear examination.	*The search* for knowledge has led *us* into ways of learning that bear examination.	Rephrased, using first person.
	People have continually sought knowledge. The search has led *them*, etc. . . .	Rewritten in two sentences.
3. man, mankind	people, humanity, human beings, humankind, human species	In this group of examples, a variety of terms may be substituted.
man's achievements	human achievements, achievements of the human species	
the average man	the average person, people in general	
man a project	staff a project, hire personnel, employ staff	
manpower	work force, personnel, workers	
Department of Manpower	(No alternative)	Official titles should not be changed.
4. The use of experiments in psychology presupposes the mechanistic nature of *man*.	The use of experiments in psychology presupposes the mechanistic nature of the *human being*.	Noun substituted.
5. This interference phenomenon, called learned helplessness, has been demonstrated in rats, cats, fish, dogs, monkeys, and *men*.	This interference phenomenon, called learned helplessness, has been demonstrated in rats, cats, fish, dogs, monkeys, and *humans*.	Noun substituted.

Examples of common usage	Consider meaning. An alternative may be better.	Comment
6. Issues raised were whether the lack of cardiac responsivity in the premature *infant* is secondary to *his* heightened level of autonomic arousal . . .	. . . responsivity in the premature *infant* is secondary to *the* heightened levels . . .	*His* changed to *the*.
	. . . responsivity in premature *infants* is secondary to *their* heightened levels . . .	Rewritten in plural.
7. First the *individual* becomes aroused by violations of *his* personal space, and then *he* attributes the cause of this arousal to other people in *his* environment.	First *we* become aroused by violations of *our* personal space, and then *we* attribute the cause of this arousal to other people in *the* environment.	Pronouns substituted, *he* and *his* omitted.
8. Much has been written about the effect that a *child's* position among *his* siblings has on *his* intellectual development.	Much has been written about the relationship between sibling position and intellectual development in *children*.	Rewritten, plural introduced.
9. Subjects were 16 girls and 16 boys. Each *child* was to place a car on *his board* so that two cars and boards looked alike.	Each child was to place a car on *his or her* board so that two cars and boards looked alike.	Changed *his* to *his or her*; however, use sparingly to avoid monotonous repetition. *Her or his* may also be used, but it sounds awkward. In either case, keep pronoun order consistent to avoid ambiguity.
10. Each person's alertness was measured by the difference between *his* obtained relaxation score and *his* obtained arousal score.	Each person's alertness was measured by the difference between *the* obtained relaxation and arousal scores.	*His* deleted, plural introduced.
11. The client's husband *lets* her teach part-time.	The client's husband *"lets"* her teach part-time. The husband says he *"lets"* the client teach part-time. The client *says her husband "lets"* her teach part-time.	Punctuation added to clarify location of the bias, that is, with husband and wife, not with author. If necessary, rewrite to clarify as allegation. See Example 24 below.

Examples of common usage	Consider meaning. An alternative may be better.	Comment
	B. *Stereotyping*	
12. males, females	men, women, boys, girls, adults, children, adolescents	Specific nouns reduce possibility of sterotypic bias and often clarify discussion. Use *male* and *female* as adjectives where appropriate and relevant (female experimenter, male subject). Avoid unparallel usages such as 10 *men* and 16 *females*.
13. Research scientists often neglect their *wives* and *children*.	Research scientists often neglect their *families*.	Alternative wording acknowledges that women as well as men are research scientists.
14. When a *test developer or test user* fails to satisfy these requirements, *he* should . . .	When *test developers or test users* fail to satisfy these requirements, *they* should . . .	Same as Example 13.
15. the psychologist . . . *he*	psychologists . . . *they*; the psychologist . . . *she*	Be specific or change to plural if discussing women as well as men.
the therapist . . . *he*	therapists . . . *they*; the therapist . . . *she*	
the nurse . . . *she*	nurses . . . *they*; nurse . . . *he*	
the teacher . . . *she*	teachers . . . *they*; teacher . . . *he*	
16. woman doctor, lady lawyer, male nurse	doctor, physician, lawyer, nurse	Specify sex if it is a variable or if sex designation is necessary to the discussion ("13 female doctors and 22 male doctors").
17. mothering	parenting, nurturing (or specify exact behaviour)	Noun substituted.

Examples of common usage	Consider meaning. An alternative may be better.	Comment
18. chairman (of an academic department)	Use *chairperson* or *chair* if it is known that the institution has established either form as an official title. Otherwise use *chairman*.	*Department head* may be appropriate, but the term is not synonymous with *chairman* and *chairperson* at all institutions.
chairman (presiding officer of a committee or meeting)	chairperson, moderator, discussion leader	In parliamentary usage *chairman* is the official term. Alternatives are acceptable in most writing.
19. Only *freshman* were eligible for the project.		
All the students had matriculated for three years, but the majority were still *freshmen*.	(No alternative if academic standing is meant.)	*First-year student* is often an acceptable alternative to *freshman*, but in these cases, *freshmen* is used for accuracy.
20. foreman, policeman, stewardess, mailman	supervisor, police officer, flight attendant, postal worker or letter carrier	Noun substituted.

II. *Problems of Evaluation*

Examples of common usage	Consider meaning. An alternative may be better.	Comment
	A. *Ambiguity of Referent*	
21. The authors acknowledge the assistance of *Mrs. John Smith*.	The authors acknowledge the assistance of *Jane Smith*.	Use given names in author acknowledgements. When forms of address are used in text, use the appropriate form: Mr., Mrs., Miss, or Ms.
22. men and women, sons and daughters, boys and girls, husbands and wives.	women and men, daughters and sons, girls and boys, wives and husbands	Vary the order if content does not require traditional order.
	B. *Stereotyping*	
23. men and girls	men and women, women and men	Use parallel terms. Of course, use *men and girls* if that is literally what is meant.

Examples of common usage	Consider meaning. An alternative may be better.	Comment
24. The client's husband lets her teach part-time.	The client teaches part-time.	The author of this example intended to communicate the working status of the woman but inadvertently revealed a stereotype about husband-wife relationships; see Example 11 above.
25. ambitious men and aggressive women	ambitious women and men or ambitious people aggressive men and women or aggressive people	Some adjectives, depending on whether the person described is a man or a woman, connote bias. The examples illustrate some common usages that may
cautious men and timid women	cautious women and men, cautious people timid men and women or timid people	not always convey exact meaning, especially when paired, as in column 1.
26. The boys chose typically male toys.	The boys chose (specify)	Being specific reduces possibility of stereotypic bias.
The client's behaviour was typically female	The client's behaviour was (specify)	
27. woman driver	driver	If specifying sex is necessary use *female driver*.
28. The *girls* in the office greeted all clients.	secretaries. office assistants	Noun substituted.
29. coed	female student	Noun substituted.
30. women's lib, women's libber	women's movement, feminist, supporter of women's movement	Noun substituted.
31. Subjects were 16 men and 4 women. *The women were housewives.*	The men were (specify) and the women were (specify).	Describe women and men in parallel terms. *Housewife* indicates sex, marital status, and occupation, and excludes men. *Homemaker* indicates occupation, and includes men.

A Final Word

Attempting to introduce nonsexist language at the cost of awkwardness, obscurity, or euphemistic phrasing does not improve scientific communication. An author should make clear that both sexes are under discussion when they are and should indicate sex when only one sex is discussed. Under no circumstances should an author hide sex identity in an attempt to be unbiased, if knowledge of sex may be important to the reader.

Any endeavour to change the language is an awesome task at best. Some aspects of our language that may be considered sexist are firmly embedded in our culture, and we presently have no acceptable substitutes. In English, the use of third-person singular pronouns is one example: the generic use of *he* is misleading, *it* is inaccurate, *one* conveys a different meaning, and *he or she* can become an annoying repetition. Nevertheless, with some rephrasing and careful attention to meaning, even the generic *he* can be avoided most of the time. The result of such efforts is accurate, unbiased communication, the purpose of these guidelines.

Suggested Reading

APA Task Force on Issues of Sexual Bias in Graduate Education. Guidelines for nonsexist use of language. *American Psychologist*, 1975, **30**, 682–684.

Burr, E., Dunn, S., & Farquhar, N. *Guidelines for equal treatment of the sexes in social studies textbooks*. Los Angeles: Westside Women's Committee, 1973. (Available from Westside Women's Committee, P.O. Box 24D20, Los Angeles, California 90024.)

DeBoard, D., Fisher, A. M., Moran, M. C., & Zawodny, L. *Guidelines to promote the awareness of human potential*. Philadelphia, Pa.: Lippincott, undated.

Harper & Row. *Harper & Row guidelines on equal treatment of the sexes in textbooks*. New York: Author, 1976.

Henley, N., & Thorne, B. *She said/he said: An annotated bibliography of sex differences in language, speech, and nonverbal communication*. Pittsburgh, Pa.: Know, 1975. (Available from Know, Inc., P.O. Box 86031, Pittsburgh, Pennsylvania 15221.)

Holt, Rinehart & Winston (College Department). *The treatment of sex roles and minorities*. New York: Author, 1976.

Lakoff, R. *Language and woman's place*. New York: Harper & Row, 1975.

Lerner, H. E. "Girls, ladies or women? The unconscious dynamics of language choice." *Comprehensive Psychiatry*, 1976, **17**, 295–299.

McGraw-Hill. *Guidelines for equal treatment of the sexes in McGraw-Hill Book Company publications*. New York: Author, undated.

Miller, C., & Swift, K. *Words and women*. Garden City, N.Y.: Anchor Press/Doubleday, 1976.

Prentice-Hall. *Prentice-Hall author's guide* (5th ed.) Englewood Cliffs, N.J.: Author, 1975.

Random House. *Guidelines for multiethnic/nonsexist survey*. New York: Author, 1975.

Scott, Foresman. *Guidelines for improving the image of women in textbooks*. Glenview, Ill.: Author, 1974.

John Wiley & Sons. *Wiley guidelines on sexism in language*. New York: Author, 1977.

This change sheet was prepared by the APA Publication Manual Task Force. Members of the task force are Charles N. Cofer (Chairperson), Robert S. Daniel, Frances Y. Dunham, and Walter I. Heimer. Ellen Kimmel served as liaison from the Committee on Women is Psychology, and Anita DeVivo as APA staff liaison. This material may be reproduced in whole or in part without permission, provided that acknowledgement is made to the American Psychological Association.